BIRDS OF THE
NATIONAL PARKS

VOËLS ▮▮ OISEAUX ▮▮ VÖGEL

Struik Publishers (Pty) Ltd
(a member of The Struik Publishing Group (Pty) Ltd)
Cornelis Struik House
80 McKenzie Street
Cape Town 8001

Reg.No: 54/00965/07

ENGLISH TEXT: Ian Davidson
AFRIKAANS TRANSLATOR: Helena van Zyl
GERMAN TRANSLATOR: Friedel Herrmann
GERMAN EDITOR: Gudrun Grapow
FRENCH TRANSLATOR: Joyce Trocki
IN-HOUSE EDITOR: Ilze Bezuidenhout
DESIGNER: Bettina Bard

Typesetting by Struik DTP, Cape Town
Reproduced by Hirt & Carter (Pty) Ltd, Cape Town
Printed and bound by Kyodo Printing Co (Pte) Ltd, Singapore

PHOTOGRAPHIC CREDITS: Nigel Dennis/SIL – pp 1, 15, 17, 21, 23, 25, 27, 29, 31, 33, 35, 41, 43, 45, 57, 61, 63, 67, 69, 75, 89, 101, 105, 107, 119, 121, 133, 139, 143, 155, 159, front cover (bottom left), title page; Nigel Dennis – pp 83, 117, front cover (top right, bottom right); David Steele/Photo Access – pp 109, 125; Terry Carew/Photo Access – p 77; S.C. Hendriks – pp 79, 91, 153; Lex Hes/Photo Access – pp 81, 145; J.J. Brooks/Photo Access – pp 71, 111, 115, 123, 131, 141, 147; J. Sneesby/Photo Access – p 73; P.J. Ginn – p 13; Ian Davidson - p 39; A. Wilson – p 59; HPH – /Photo Access – pp 47, 53, 113, 127, 135; D. Smeerdijk/Photo Access – p 137; Peter Pickford/SIL – pp 49, 65, 85, 92, 95, 97, 99, 149, front cover (top left); Jean Laurie/Photo Access – p 151; J.F. Carlyon/Photo Access – pp 87, 157; Peter Steyn/Photo Access – pp 11, 19, 37, 51, 129; J&B Photographers/Photo Access – p 55; GPL du Plessis/ Photo Access – p 103.

ISBN 1 86825 873 4

FRONT COVER: *(clockwise from top left)* Little Bee-eater; Bateleur; Blackheaded Oriole; Southern Yellowbilled Stork

CONTENTS

FOREWORD

Although birds know no boundaries, our national parks can be regarded as 'bird islands' – sanctuaries where the diversity of species are safe, havens where they can feed, breed and nest, or stop over along long migration routes. The multiplicity of our birdlife is reflected in the diversity of the 17 national parks.

This book challenges bird-lovers to spot the 75 species most commonly found in our national parks – from the Kruger National Park with its wealth of birds to the waders of the West Coast National Park.

We have numerous wetlands in our national parks as well as two Ramsar sites (Wetlands of International Importance), one in the Wilderness National Park and the other in the West Coast National Park. These areas are extremely important as they assist the conservation efforts of countries in the North.

In conclusion, I would like to thank Struik Publishers for their assistance in making visitors to the national parks more aware of the avifauna.

Dr. G.A. Robinson
Chief Executive
National Parks Board

VOORWOORD

Hoewel voëls nie deur grense beperk word nie, kan Suid-Afrika se nasionale parke beskou word as 'voëleilande' – skuilplekke waar die diversiteit van spesies beskerm word, toevlugsoorde waar hulle kan vreet, broei en nesmaak of aandoen terwyl hulle migreer. Die veelvuldigheid van ons voëllewe word weerspieël deur die diversiteit binne die 17 nasionale parke.

Hierdie boek daag voëlliefhebbers uit om die 75 spesies wat algemeen in ons nasionale parke aangetref word, uit te ken. Hoewel verskeie vleilande in ons nasionale parke voorkom, het ons ook twee Ramsar-terreine (Vleilande van Internasionale Belang) – in die Wildernis Nasionale Park en in die Weskus Nasionale Park. Hierdie gebiede is belangrik omdat hulle bydra tot die bewaringspogings van lande in die Noorde.

Ter afsluiting wil ek Struik Uitgewers bedank vir hulle bydrae om besoekers aan die nasionale parke meer bewus te maak van voëls.

Dr. G.A. Robinson
Hoof Uitvoerende Direkteur
Nasionale Parkeraad

PREFACE

Bien que les oiseaux ne connaîssent nulles frontières, les parcs nationaux de l'Afrique du Sud sont des 'îles d'oiseaux' – des refuges où les espèces sont sans danger, des asiles pour nicher ou séjourner le long des routes de migration.

Ce livre invite les amateurs d'oiseaux à reconnaître les 75 espèces les plus générales qui se trouvent dans les parcs nationaux – du Parc national Kruger, qui seul possede deux-tiers du nombre d'espèces de toute l'Australie, aux échassiers du Parc national West Coast.

Le pays a aussi deux endroits Ramsar (Marécages d'Importance Internationale), l'un au Parc national Wilderness, l'autre au Parc national West Coast. Ces régions importantes aident les tentatives de conservation des pays du Nord.

En conclusion, je voudrais remercier Struik Publishers d'avoir aidé les visiteurs aux parcs nationaux mieux connaître la biodiversité en général, et l'avi-faune en particulier dans ce cas.

Dr G.A. Robinson
Directeur en chef
Comité des Parcs nationaux

VORWORT

Vögel kennen keine Grenzen, aber die Nationalparks in Südafrika sind dennoch 'Inseln der Vogelwelt' – Schutzgebiete, wo sich die Vielfalt der Arten in einem passendem Umfeld entfalten kann, wo Vögel sich der Nahrungssuche, der Fortpflanzung und der Aufzucht ihrer Jungen widmen, und wo sie auf ihren langen Wanderzügen rasten können. In den 17 Nationalparks präsentiert sich die breite Palette unseres reichen Vogellebens.

Dieses Buch ist eine Anregung für den Vogelliebhaber, die 75 Vogelarten, die in unseren Nationalparks am häufigsten vorkommen, zu erkennen. Allein der Kruger-Nationalpark kommt auf etwa Zweidrittel der Anzahl der Vogelarten, die ganz Australien aufzuweisen hat; hinzu kommen noch die anderen Schutzgebiete.

Ich möchte hiermit Struik Publishers meinen Dank für ihren Beitrag aussprechen, der den Besuchern unserer Nationalparks die südafrikanische Vogelwelt bewußter werden läßt.

Dr G.A. Robinson
Vorstanvorsitzender
National Parks Board

INTRODUCTION

Birds of the National Parks covers 75 of the most common and obvious bird species found in the 17 national parks. Each description is accompanied by a silhouette of the species, a symbol of its habitat requirements and a list of the national parks where it could occur.

The description applies to adult birds; immatures are described only where relevant. Facts relating to its habitat, food requirements, call and habits provide the reader with background information on each species. The habitat symbol shows the environment where a bird may occur in its broadest sense. These habitats are open woodlands, inland freshwaters, coastal waters and grasslands (which can include agricultural land).

Open woodlands cover a range of wooded country, from open, dry grasslands with scattered trees to the more densely bushed thornveld in the north-eastern parts of the country. Inland freshwaters include rivers, lakes, pans, dams, estuaries and marshlands or flooded grasslands. Grasslands (agricultural lands) may have the occasional tree, but vary from long grass, in the moister, eastern sector of the country to short grass in the more arid western parts of the country. Coastal waters include ocean shorelines.

INLEIDING

Hierdie boekie dek 75 van die algemeenste voëlspesies wat in die 17 nasionale parke aangetref word. Elke beskrywing word vergesel van 'n profiel van die spesie, 'n diagrammatiese voorstelling van die habitatvereistes en 'n lys van die nasionale parke waar die spesie voorkom.

Die spesiebeskrywing is van toepassing op volwasse voëls; onvolwassenes word net beskryf waar nodig. Inligting soos habitatvoorkeure, kosvereistes, roep en gewoontes gee die leser agtergrondinligting oor elke spesie. 'n Voël se habitat is 'n belangrike aspek van voëlidentifikasie. Dit is onwaarskynlik dat 'n mens spesies wat afhanklik is van water, soos pikkewyne, visvangers en reiers, op 'n ander plek as naby water sal aantref. Die habitatvoorstelling dui die omgewing waar 'n voël kan voorkom in die breedste sin aan. Oop boswêreld dek 'n spektrum beboste dele – van oop, droë grasvelde met 'n paar bome tot die digter beboste doringveld in die noordooste van die land. Binnelandse varswatergebiede sluit riviere, mere, panne, damme, mondings en moerasse of oorstroomde grasvelde in. Hoewel daar op grasvelde (en landerye) soms 'n paar bome voorkom, wissel dit van lang gras in die vogtiger oostelike deel van die land tot kort gras in die droër westelike dele van die land. Kuswater sluit die kuslyn in.

INTRODUCTION

Les Oiseaux des Parcs Nationaux décrit 75 des espèces d'oiseau les plus frappantes et les plus fréquentes des 17 parcs nationaux de l'Afrique du Sud. Chaque description a une silhouette de l'espèce, un symbole qui indique les besoins de son habitat et une liste des parcs nationaux où elle peut se trouver.

La description s'applique aux oiseaux adultes; on décrit les immatures seulement quand c'est applicable. Les détails concernant l'habitat, les besoins en nourriture, le cri et les habitudes donnent au lecteur des données de base pour chaque espèce. L'environnement où l'oiseau peut se rencontrer comprend les pays boisés découverts, les eaux douces de l'intérieur, les eaux côtières et les prairies (les terres agricoles).

Les pays boisés découverts veut dire une étendue de pays boisés, des prairies découvertes et sèches à quelques arbres, à l'épine, et à la brousse plus épaisse du nord-est de l'Afrique du Sud. Les eaux douces de l'intérieur du pays comprend les rivières, les lacs, les bassins, les barrages, les estuaires et les marais ou les prairies inondées. Les prairies (les terres agricoles) varient de l'herbe longue de l'est plus humide à l'herbe courte de l'ouest plus sec. Les eaux côtières comprennent les rivages.

EINLEITUNG

Dieses Buch behandelt über 75 der verbreitetsten und auffälligsten Vogelarten, die in den 17 Nationalparks vorkommen. Zu jeder Beschreibung eines Vogels gibt es eine Silhouette der Spezies, ein Symbol für seine Nistbedürfnisse und eine Liste der Nationalparks, in denen man den Vogel wahrscheinlich antrifft.

Die Beschreibung bezieht sich auf das Schlichtkleid des ausgewachsenen Vogels; wo es angemessen ist, werden auch Jungvögel beschrieben. Einzelheiten bezüglich des Habitats, der Nahrungsbedürfnisse, der Rufe und der Gewohnheiten vermitteln dem Leser ein Basiswissen über jede Spezies. Das Symbol für das Habitat weist das Umfeld, die Umgebung aus, wo man diesen Vogel antreffen kann. Es handelt sich um Dornsavannen, Binnengewässer, Küstengewässer, Grasland und Grasfluren (landwirtschaftliches Gebiet).

Die Dornsavanne beinhaltet eine weite Skala Baumlandschaft, von offener Trockensavanne mit vereinzelten Bäumen bis zu den dichten Dickichten im Nordosten des Landes. Binnengewässer schließen Flüsse, Seen, Salzpfannen, Stauseen, Ästuarien, Sümpfe sowie überflutete Grasebenen ein. Grasfluren können auch vereinzelte Bäume enthalten, wechseln aber von hohem Gras in den feuchteren Gebiete im Osten bis zu dem kurzen Gras im Westen des Landes.

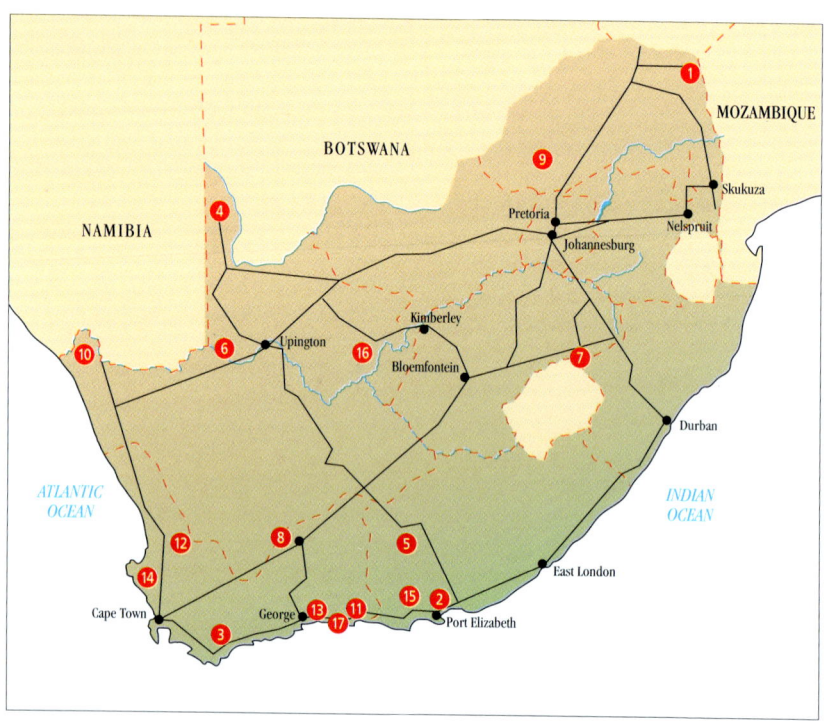

1. Kruger National Park

2. Addo Elephant National Park

3. Bontebok National Park

4. Kalahari Gemsbok
   National Park

5. Mountain Zebra National Park

6. Augrabies Falls National Park

7. Golden Gate Highlands
   National Park

8. Karoo National Park

9. Marakele National Park

10. Richtersveld National Park

11. Tsitsikamma National Park

12. Tankwa Karoo National Park

13. Wilderness National Park

14. West Coast National Park

15. Addo Elephant National Park
    (formerly Zuurberg National Park)

16. \Hei-!gariep National Park

17. Knysna National Lake Area

Key to symbols/Simboolsleutel/Symbolerklärung/Légende

 PROFILE/PROFIEL/SILHOUETTE/PROFIL

 COASTAL WATERS/KUSGEBIEDE/KÜSTENGEWÄSSER/EAUX CÔTIÈRES

 GRASSLAND/GRASVELD/GRASLAND/PRAIRIES

 INLAND FRESHWATER/BINNELANDSE VARSWATERGEBIEDE/
BINNENGEWÄSSER/EAUX DOUCES DE L'INTÉRIEUR

 WOODLANDS/BOSWÊRELD/DORNSAVANNE/
PAYS BOISÉS DÉCOUVERTS

 REEDBEDS/RIETBEDDINGS/SCHILF/ROSLIÈRES

 ROCKY TERRAIN/ROTSAGTIGE GEBIEDE/FELSIGES GEBIET/
TERRAIN ROCHEUX

KRUGER,
BONTEBOK,
KAROO

NATIONAL PARKS WHERE BIRDS CAN BE FOUND/NASIONALE
PARKE WAAR VOËLS AANGETREF WORD/NATIONALPARKS, IN DENEN
VÖGEL LEBEN/DES PARCS NATIONAUX OÙ ON PEUT TROUVER DES
OISEAUX

Spheniscus demersus

JACKASS PENGUIN (3)

The adult Jackass Penguin shows a black and white facial pattern, pale belly and pink eye ring. Immatures are greyish brown and lack the breast band seen in adults. This species occurs only along the southern African coasts, where it breeds mostly on offshore islands. Its common name is derived from the call, a loud donkey-like braying sound, often uttered at night.

BRILPIKKEWYN (3)

Die volwasse Brilpikkewyn vertoon 'n swart-en-wit gesigspatroon, bleek pens en pienk oogring. Onvolwassenes is grysbruin en het nie die grys borsband van die volwasse voël nie. Die Engelse naam is afgelei van hulle roep wat veral snags geuiter word en klink soos die harde gebalk van 'n donkie. Hulle kom slegs voor langs die kus van suidelike Afrika waar hulle meestal naby kuseilande broei.

LE MANCHOT DU CAP (3)

Le dessin facial de l'adulte manchot du Cap est noir et blanc, le ventre est pâle et le cerne est rose. Les immatures sont brun gris et ils, manquent la bande de poitrine des adultes. Cette espèce ne se rencontre que le long des côtes africaines du sud, où elle se reproduit surtout sur les îles côtières. Le cri estun bruit retentissant qui ressemble au braiment d'un âne et qui s'entend souvent la nuit.

BRILLENPINGUIN (3)

Der ausgewachsene Brillenpinguin hat eine schwarzweiße Gesichtszeichnung, einen hellen Bauch und rosa Augenring. Der Jungvogel ist gräulichbraun, ohne das Brustband des ausgewachsenen Vogels. Diese Art kommt nur an der Küste des südlichen Afrika vor, wo sie hauptsächlich auf vorgelagerten Inseln nistet. Der englische Name (Jackass Penguin) ist von dem lauten, eselartigen Schrei abgeleitet, der oft des Nachts ausgestoßen wird.

Spheniscus demersus

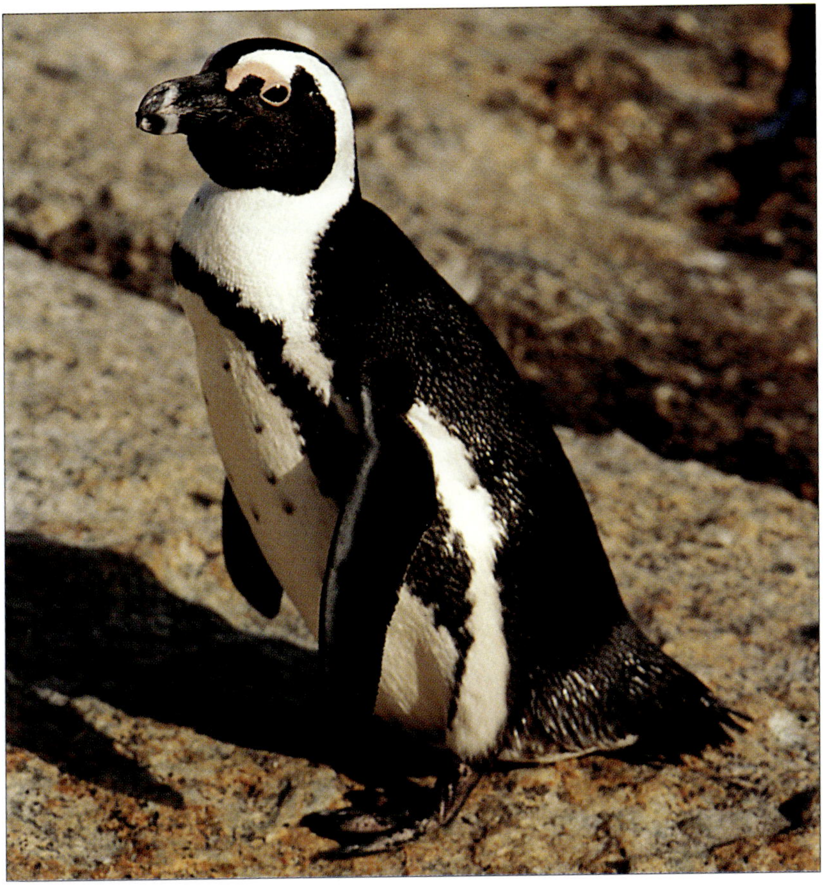

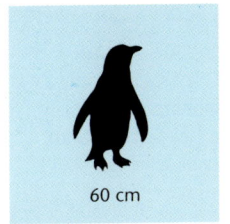

60 cm

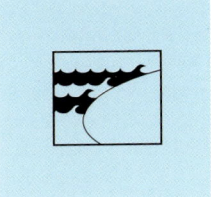

West Coast,
Wilderness

Tachybaptus ruficollis

DABCHICK (8)

These small waterbirds have a chestnut-coloured neck and, in the adult, a clear white to cream spot at the base of the bill. Immatures are paler and show a whitish neck. They are commonly seen on open stretches of fresh water. Fledglings travel on the backs of the adults, remaining there even when the adults dive below to feed on aquatic insects, tadpoles and frogs.

KLEINDOBBERTJIE (8)

Hierdie klein watervoël het 'n kastaiingbruin nek; by volwassenes kom 'n duidelike wit tot ligroomkleurige kol aan die snawelbasis voor. Onvolwassenes is bleker en vertoon 'n witterige nek. Hulle word gewoonlik in groot getalle gesien by oop plate varswater. Die kuikens verlaat die nes na hulle uitgebroei het en reis op die rûe van die volwasse voëls.

LE GREBE CASTAGNEUX (8)

Ces petits oiseaux d'eau ont le cou châtain. L'adulte a une tache blanche à crème au bas du bec. Les immatures sont plus pâles et ont le cou blanc. Ils se voient généralement aux grandes étendues de l'eau fraîche, à la végétation émergente, et souvent en grand nombre. Les oisillons quittent le nid après l'éclosion. Ils voyagent à dos des adultes, et y restent quand les adultes plongent sous l'eau pour manger des insectes aquatiques, des têtards et des crapauds.

ZWERGTAUCHER (8)

Diese kleinen Wasservögel haben einen kastanienfarbenen Nacken und im Schlichtkleid einen weißen bis cremefarbenen Fleck in der Schnabelwurzel. Das Jugendkleid ist heller, mit weißlichem Hals. Diese Vögel trifft man häufig und zahlreich auf offenen Süßwassern. Jungvögel hocken selbst beim Tauchen auf dem Rücken der ausgewachsenen Vögel, und verharren auch dann dort, wenn die großen Vögel untertauchen, um sich von Wasserinsekten zu ernähren.

Tachybaptus ruficollis

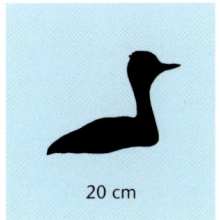

20 cm

Addo Elephant, Bontebok, Golden Gate Highlands, Kalahari Gemsbok, Karoo, Knysna National Lake Area, Kruger, Marakele, Tankwa Karoo, Mountain Zebra, Richtersveld, Tsitsikamma, Augrabies Falls, \Hei-!Gariep, West Coast, Wilderness

Pelecanus onocrotalus

EASTERN WHITE PELICAN (49)

This unmistakable large bird is white with black flight feathers; the white feathers assume a pinkish flush during the breeding season. The bright yellow pouch hanging below the long pinkish bill is used to catch fish. Immatures are dark brown to grey in colour, depending on their age. They may be seen in freshwater or saltwater estuaries, lagoons and dams, feeding in groups on fish.

WITPELIKAAN (49)

Die Witpelikaan, onmiskenbaar vanweë sy enorme grootte, is wit met swart vliegvere wat 'n pienkerige kleur aanneem gedurende die broeiseisoen. Die heldergeel snawelsak wat onder die lang, pienkerige snawel hang, word gebruik om vis mee te vang. Onvolwassenes is eers donkerbruin en word later grys. Hulle kom voor by vars- of seewatermondings waar hulle skole visse vang.

LE PELICAN BLANC ORIENTAL (49)

Facile à reconnaître à cause de sa grande taille, ce pélican blanc a les plumes de vol noires qui deviennent rosâtres pendant la saison de reproduction. La poche ventrale jaune sous le bec long et rosâtre s'utilise pour attraper les poissons. Les immatures sont brun foncé à gris, selon l'âge. On voit cette espèce aux estuaires d'eau douce ou saline, aux lagunes et aux barrages, se nourrissant en groupes aux bancs voyageurs.

ROSAPELIKAN (49)

Das Gefieder des Rosapelikans ist weiß, die schwarzen Schwungfedern nehmen zur Brutzeit eine rosa Färbung an, und er ist durch seine Größe unverkennbar. Der grellgelbe Kehlsack, der sich unterhalb des langen, hellrosa Schnabels befindet, dient dem Fischfang. Jungvögel rangieren farblich von Dunkelbraun bis Grau, je nach Alter. Man trifft sie an Süßwasser- oder Salzwasserästuarien, Lagunen und Stauseen an; bei Fischschwärmen treten sie scharenweise auf.

Pelecanus onocrotalus

180 cm

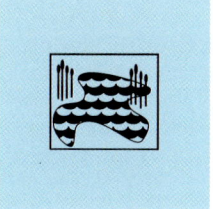

Kruger,
West Coast

Phalacrocorax africanus

REED CORMORANT (58)

These birds are often seen perched out of the water with their wings outstretched. Adults are dark brown in colour with a yellow bill and a red eye. Immatures are lighter and show a white breast and belly. A widespread and common aquatic species, it can be found on freshwater dams, lakes and rivers. Reed Cormorants feed on fish and frogs and may roost in large groups.

RIETDUIKER (58)

Rietduikers word dikwels gesien waar hulle buite die water sit met uitgespreide vlerke. Volwasse voëls is donkerbruin met 'n geel snawel en 'n rooi oog. Onvolwassenes is ligter en vertoon 'n wit bors en pens. Hierdie algemene waterspesie kom wydverspreid voor en word by varswaterdamme, -mere en riviere aangetref. Hulle leef van vis en paddas, en slaap soms in groot groepe.

LE CORMORAN DE ROSEAUX (58)

Le cormoran de roseaux perche souvent hors de l'eau, les ailes étendues. Les adultes sont brun foncé et ils ont le bec jaune et l'oeil rouge. Les immatures, qui sont plus clairs, ont la poitrine et le ventre blancs. On trouve cette espèce aquatique, fréquente et répandue, près des barrages d'eau douce, des lacs et des rivières. Cet oiseau se nourrit de poissons et de crapauds et ils se juchent quelquefois en grandes groupes.

RIEDSCHARBE (58)

Diese Vögel kann man oft mit ausgestreckten Flügeln außerhalb des Wassers hocken sehen. Ausgewachsen haben sie ein dunkelbraunes Gefieder, einen gelben Schnabel und rote Augen. Das Jugendkleid ist heller, mit weißer Brust und weißem Bauch. Man trifft diesen weitverbreiteten Wasservogel an Stauseen, Binnenseen und Flüssen an. Er ernährt sich von Fischen und Fröschen und nistet mitunter in großen Schwärmen.

52 cm

ADDO ELEPHANT, BONTEBOK,
GOLDEN GATE HIGHLANDS,
KALAHARI GEMSBOK, KAROO,
KNYSNA NATIONAL LAKE AREA,
KRUGER, MARAKELE, TANKWA KAROO,
MOUNTAIN ZEBRA, RICHTERSVELD,
TSITSIKAMMA, AUGRABIES FALLS,
\HEI-!GARIEP, WEST COAST,
WILDERNESS

Ardea melanocephala

BLACKHEADED HERON (63)

Adults have a dark head and neck, which help to differentiate them from other large grey herons and cranes. Immatures are greyer than adults and have a grey head and neck, and black legs. These large crane-like bird are often seen striding about in open grasslands, agricultural fields and, especially, recently burnt areas where they search for insects, mice, snakes and lizards.

SWARTKOPREIER (63)

Volwasse voëls het 'n donker kop en nek, wat help om hulle te onderskei van ander groot, grys reiers en kraanvoëls. Onvolwassenes is gryser; hulle het 'n grys kop en nek, en swart bene. Hierdie groot, kraanvoëlagtige spesie word dikwels gesien waar dit loop oor oop grasveld en pas afgebrande gebiede, op soek na insekte, muise, slange en akkedisse. Die roep is 'n harde 'aaaaaaark'.

LE HERON A TETE NOIRE (63)

Les adultes sont différents d'autres grands hérons et des grues, ayant la tête et le cou noirs. Les immatures plus gris ont les pattes noires, la tête et le cou souvent gris. Ce grand oiseau se voit souvent marchant à grands pas dans les prairies découvertes, dans les champs agricoles et surtout dans des régions récemment brûlées où ils cherchent des insectes, des souris, des serpents et des lézards. Le cri est un 'aaark' haut et couic.

SCHWARZKOPFREIHER (63)

Von anderen großen, grauen Reihern und Kranichen unterscheidet sich dieser durch den schwarzen Kopf und schwarzen Nacken. Das Jugendkleid ist grauer, Kopf und Nacken sind auch grau, die Läufe schwarz. Der Ruf ist ein lautes, heiseres 'Aaark'. Den großen, kranichartigen Vogel sieht man auf offenen Grasfluren und Feldern herumstelzen, besonders in kürzlich abgebrannten Gegenden, wo er Insekten, Mäuse, Schlangen und Eidechsen sucht.

Ardea melanocephala

96 cm

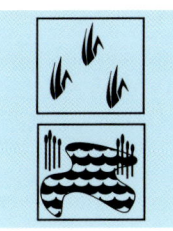

Addo Elephant, Bontebok, Golden Gate Highlands, Kalahari Gemsbok, Karoo, Knysna National Lake Area, Kruger, Marakele, Tankwa Karoo, Mountain Zebra, Richtersveld, Tsitsikamma, Augrabies Falls, \Hei-!Gariep, West Coast, Wilderness

Bubulcus ibis

CATTLE EGRET (71)

An abundant, cosmopolitan species, this small heron is mostly non-aquatic. Adults show a buffy breast and crown; when breeding, the yellow bill and legs change to a deeper orange colour. Immatures are white with dark legs and a yellow bill. This bird is often seen riding on the backs of cattle and elephants. It feeds on insects flushed by grazing animals. The call is a heron-like 'kraak'.

BOSLUISVOËL (71)

Hierdie klein, wit reierspesie is volop en meestal nie-waterlewend. Volwasse voëls het 'n liggeel bors en kroon; tydens broeityd verander die geel snawel en bene na 'n dieper oranjekleur. Onvolwassenes is wit met donker bene en 'n geel snawel. Hulle word gewoonlik gesien waar hulle op die rûe van wilde en plaasdiere ry. Hulle vang insekte wat opgejaag word deur diere wat wei.

L'AIGRETTE DE BETAIL (71)

Une espèce abondante et cosmopolite, ce petit héron blanc est surtout non-aquatique. Il a la poitrine et la couronne chamois; en saison de reproduction le bec et les pattes orangés sont plus sombres. Les immatures blancs ont les pattes sombres et le bec jaune. Il se voit souvent parmi de grands groupes d'animaux sauvages et domestiques, se promenant quelquefois à dos d'un grand animal. Il se nourrit d'insectes excrétés. Le cri ressemble au 'kraak' du héron.

KUHREIHER (71)

Dieser kleine, weiße Reiher ist weltweit verbreitet und nicht an Gewässer gebunden. Scheitel und Brust des ausgewachsenen Vogels sind bräunlich; im Brutkleid verändert sich das Gelb des Schnabels und der Läufe in ein dunkleres Orange. Das Jugendkleid ist weiß, mit dunklen Läufen und gelbem Schnabel. Diese Art folgt oft scharenweise dem Wild oder Vieh und ernährt sich von Insekten, die von den weidenden Tieren aufgestört werden.

Bubulcus ibis

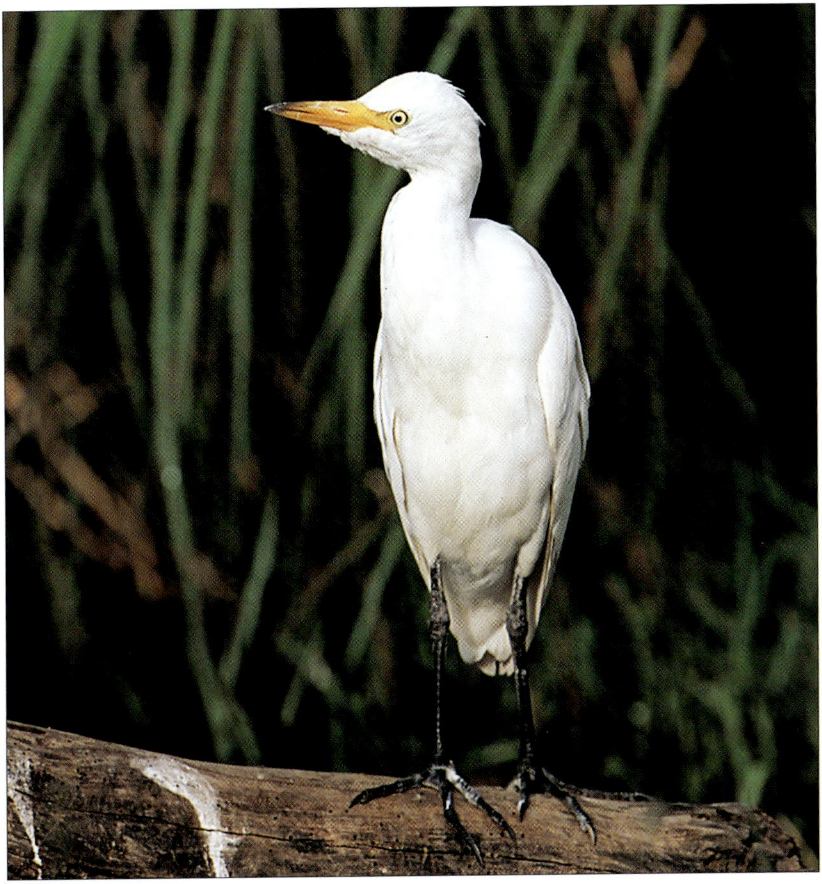

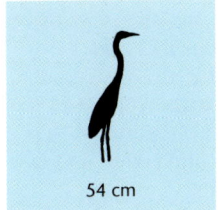

54 cm

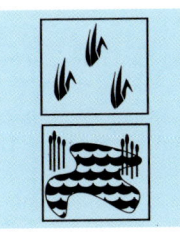

ADDO ELEPHANT, BONTEBOK,
GOLDEN GATE HIGHLANDS,
KNYSNA NATIONAL LAKE AREA,
KRUGER, MARAKELE,
MOUNTAIN ZEBRA,
TSITSIKAMMA,
\HEI-!GARIEP,
WEST COAST,
WILDERNESS

Scopus umbretta

HAMERKOP (81)

This dark brown, heron-like bird has a flattened bill and elongated nape feathers. Entirely African, it feeds on frogs, tadpoles and small fish. Its flight action is jerky and bouncy; it often calls 'kiep, kiep' in flight. The nest, built on a cliff face or in the fork of a large tree, is a large, dome-shaped structure made of sticks, reeds and mud; it can take up to six months to complete.

HAMERKOP (81)

Hierdie donkerbruin, reieragtige voël het 'n afgeplatte snawel en verlengde kuifvere aan die agterkop. Hulle vreet paddas, paddavisse en klein vissies. Die vliegbeweging is rukkerig en bonsend; die Hamerkop roep dikwels 'kiep, kiep' in vlug. Die nes wat op 'n kranslys of in die mik van 'n groot boom gebou word, is 'n groot, koepelvormige struktuur van stokkies, riete en modder.

L'OMBRETTE (81)

Cet oiseau brun foncé qui ressemble au héron, a le bec aplati et les plumes de nuque allongées. Il se nourrit de grenouilles, de têtards et de petits poissons. Son vol est saccadé et rebondissant et il appelle souvent 'kiep, kiep' en volant. Il construit son grand nid de bâtons, de roseaux et de boue, en forme de dôme, sur une falaise ou dans la branche fourchue d'un grand arbre; la construction dure jusqu'à six mois. On croit qu'elle peut voir l'avenir reflété dans l'eau.

HAMMERKOPF (81)

Dieser dunkelbraune, reiherartige Vogel hat einen flachen Schnabel und verlängerte Nackenfedern und kommt ausschließlich in Afrika vor; er ernährt sich von Fröschen, Kaulquappen und kleinen Fischen. Die Flugbewegung ist ruckartig, und er stößt oft ein 'Kiep-Kiep' im Flug aus. Das kuppelförmige Nest am Steilhang oder in einer Baumgabel ist aus Stöcken, Schilf und Lehm, und es kann bis zu sechs Monaten dauern, ehe es vollendet ist.

Scopus umbretta

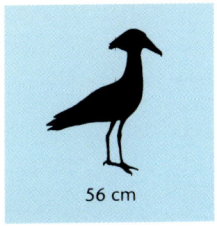

56 cm

Addo Elephant, Bontebok,
Golden Gate Highlands,
Kalahari Gemsbok, Karoo,
Knysna National Lake Area,
Kruger, Marakele, Tankwa Karoo,
Mountain Zebra, Richtersveld,
Tsitsikamma, Augrabies Falls,
\Hei-!gariep, West Coast,
Wilderness

Leptoptilos crumeniferus

MARABOU STORK (89)

The Marabou Stork, the 'ugly duckling' of the storks, is a large bird with a huge greyish-coloured bill, a naked pinkish head and a pink throat pouch which flails about in the wind when it flies. It spends much of its day standing or squatting on its 'knees'. It is most often seen in game reserves at the carcasses of predator kills, or at abattoirs and refuse dumps, often in the company of vultures.

MARABOE (89)

Die Maraboe, die lelike eendjie van die ooievare, is 'n groot voël met 'n kaal, pienkerige kop,'n massiewe, gryserige snawel, en 'n pienk keelsak wat wapper in die wind wanneer hy vlieg. Hierdie voël spandeer die grootste deel van die dag staande of gehurk op sy 'knieë'. Hulle word dikwels gesien in wildreservate by die karkasse van roofdiere se prooi of, andersins, by slagpale en vullishope.

LA CIGOGNE MARABOU (89)

Ce vilain petit canard des cigognes est un grand oiseau au bec grisâtre énorme, à la tête nue rosâtre et à la poche de cou rose qui bouge dans le vent quand il vole. Il passe la plupart de sa journée debout où accroupi sur les 'genoux'. Cette espèce se rencontre le plus souvent aux réserves naturelles, aux carcasses des mises à mort de prédateur, et aussi aux abattoirs et aux voiries. Ces oiseaux se voient souvent avec des vautours.

MARABU (89)

Der Marabu ist das 'häßliche Entlein' unter den Störchen, ein riesiger Vogel mit gewaltigem, gräulichem Schnabel, kahlem, rosa Kopf und rosafarbenem Kehlsack, der im Flug hin- und herschlabbert. Er verbringt einen Großteil des Tages im Stehen oder auf den 'Knien' hockend. Diesen Vogel trifft man hauptsächlich in Wildschutzgebieten an Kadavern von Raubwildopfern oder auch bei Schlachthöfen oder Abfallhalden an, und das oft in Begleitung von Aasgeiern.

Leptoptilos crumeniferus

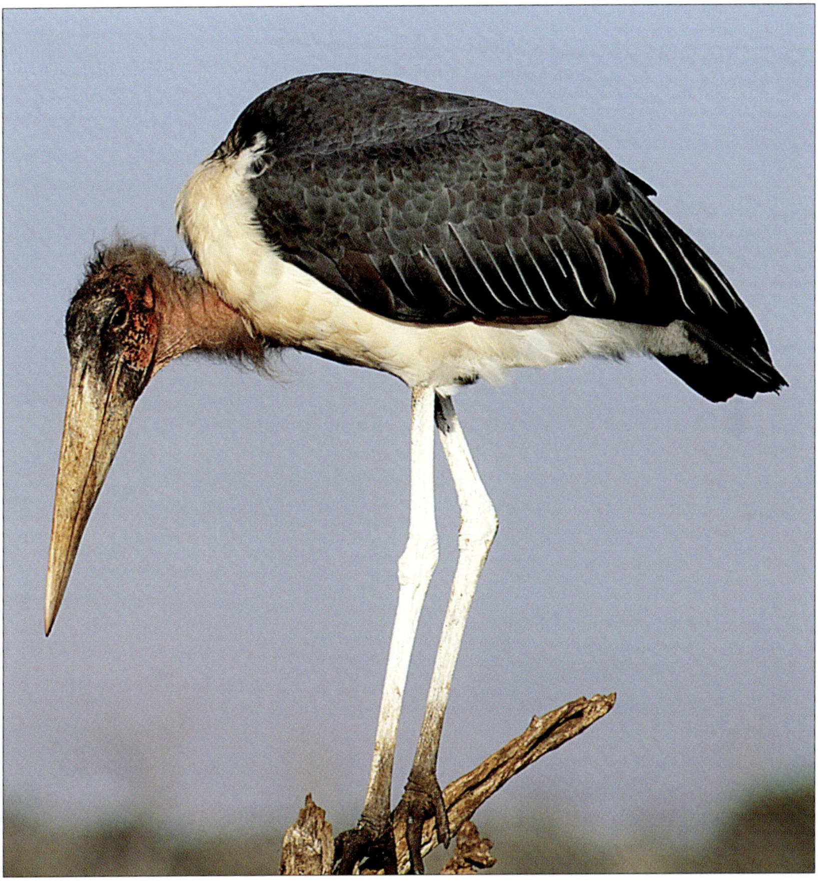

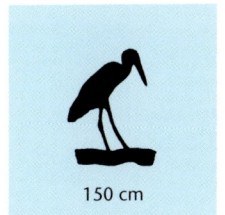

150 cm

KRUGER,
KALAHARI GEMSBOK

Threskiornis aethiopicus

SACRED IBIS (91)

These medium-sized black and white birds with their long, decurved black bills are most often seen flying across the sky in 'V' formation during the late evening and early morning. On the ground they can be seen in small groups in marshy grasslands and vleis, cultivated lands and sewage works, where they dig with their bills for insects, molluscs and frogs.

SKOORSTEENVEËR (91)

Hierdie mediumgrootte, swart-en-wit voëls wat lang, afgeboë, swart snawels het, word meestal gesien wanneer hulle vroegoggend of laataand in 'n V-formasie in die lug vlieg. Op die grond kan hulle in klein groepies gesien word in vogtige savanne en vleie, verboude landerye en watersuiweringsaanlegte waar hulle met hulle snawels grawe op soek na insekte, weekdiertjies en paddas.

L'IBIS SACRE (91)

Les ibis sacrés sont des oiseaux noirs et blancs. Ils sont de taille moyenne, aux becs noirs, longs et décourbés qui se voient le plus souvent tard le soir et tôt le matin volant en formation 'V'. Par terre, on peut voir ces oiseaux en petits groupes aux prairies, aux marais, aux marécages, aux terrres cultivées et aux systèmes d'égouts, où ils creusent du bec, cherchant des insectes, des mollusques et des grenouilles.

HEILIGER IBIS (91)

Man nimmt diese mittelgroßen, schwarzweißen Vögel, mit den langen, nach unten gekrümmten Schnäbeln am häufigsten in der Morgen- und Abenddäm-merung wahr, wenn sie in V-Formation am Himmel fliegen. Auf dem Boden trifft man diese Vögel in kleinen Schwärmen an Sümpfen und Tümpeln an, ebenso auf Felden und bei Kläranlagen, wo sie nach Insekten, Schnecken und Fröschen gründeln.

Threskiornis aethiopicus

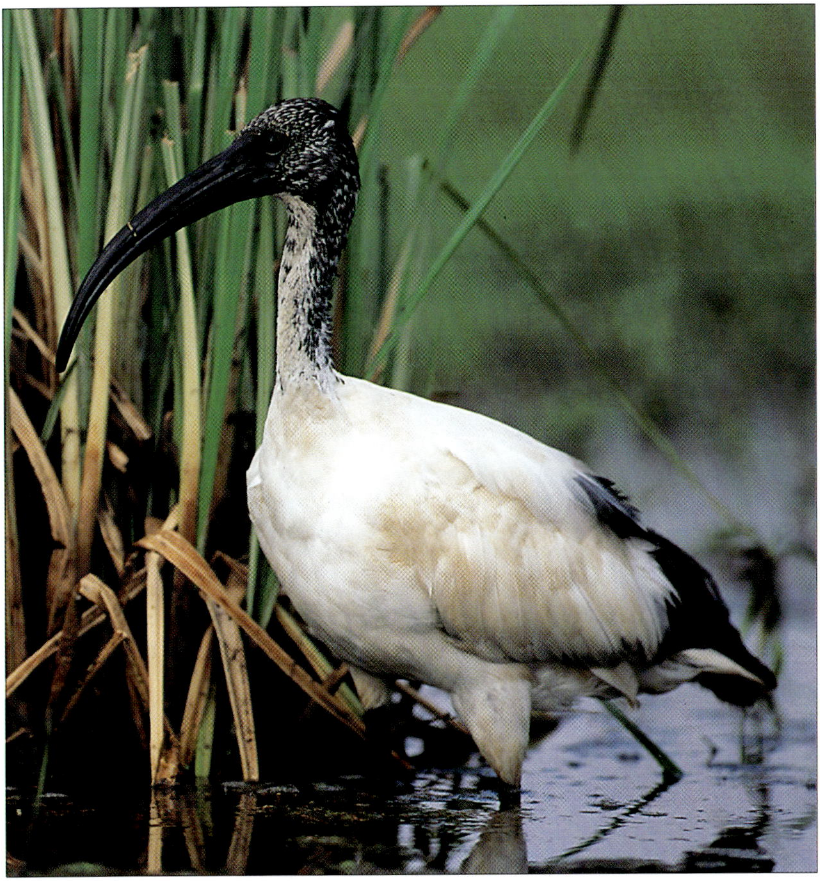

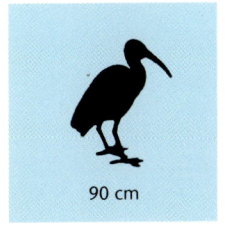

90 cm

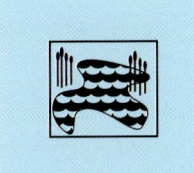

Addo Elephant,
Bontebok,
Golden Gate Highlands,
Knysna National Lake Area,
Kruger, Marakele,
Mountain Zebra,
Richtersveld, \Hei-!Gariep,
West Coast,
Wilderness

Phoenicopterus minor

LESSER FLAMINGO (97)

This long-legged, long-necked aquatic species varies in colour from pink to pinkish white. The bill and facial skin are deep red in colour. They feed by filtering micro-organisms from the water's surface with the bill held upside-down, often stirring up the bottom mud with their feet. These nomadic birds may be seen on saltwater estuaries and freshwater pans; they breed inland.

KLEINFLAMINK (97)

Hierdie langbeen, langnek waterspesie se kleur wissel van pienk tot pienkerig wit. Sy snawel en gesig het 'n dieprooi kleur. Hulle is hoogs groeplewend. Hulle vreet deur mikroörganismes van die wateroppervlak te filtreer deur hulle snawels onderstebo te hou, terwyl hulle dikwels modder van die bodem met hulle pote loswoel. Hierdie nomadiese voëls broei nie by die kus nie.

LE PETIT FLAMANT (97)

Cet oiseau aquatique à pattes et à cou longs varie de rose à blanc rosâtre. Le bec et la peau du visage sont rouge foncé. Ils sont très grégaires. Ils se nourissent en filtrant des micro-organismes à la surface de l'eau, le bec renversé, souvent en remuant des pattes la boue du fond. On peut voir ces oiseaux très nomades aux estuaires salines et aux bassins d'eau douce. Ils se reproduisent à l'intérieur sur les plaines boueuses des lacs salins. Le cri ressemble au cri de l'oie sauvage.

ZWERGFLAMINGO (97)

Dieser langbeinige, langhalsige Wasservogel rangiert farblich von rosa bis weißrosa; Schnabel und Gesichtshaut sind tiefrot. Er lebt gesellig. Flamingos sind Nomaden, die man an Salzwasserästuarien und Salzpfannen antrifft. Mit umgedrehtem Kopf seiht er Nahrungsteilchen mit dem Schnabel aus dem Wasser und wühlt dabei mit den Füßen den schlammigen Boden auf. Der Ruf klingt wie ein Gänseschrei. Sie nisten im Inland in salzhaltigen Gewässern.

Phoenicopterus minor

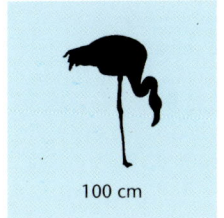

100 cm

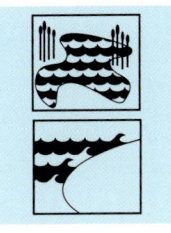

Addo Elephant, Bontebok,
Golden Gate Highlands,
Knysna National Lake Area,
Kruger, Mountain Zebra,
\Hei-!gariep,
West Coast,
Wilderness

Dendrocygna viduata

WHITEFACED DUCK (99)

Characteristically, adults have a long, black to chestnut brown neck, a brown mottled back and a white face which becomes dirty and brown from feeding in muddy waters. It dabbles for food, sometimes diving for water weed and tubers, but also feeds on grains. These gregarious birds stand erect with an outstretched neck when anxious or alarmed. The call is a whistling 'swee-swee-sweeu'.

NONNETJIE-EEND (99)

Volwasse voëls het 'n kenmerkende lang, swart tot kastaiingbruin nek, 'n bruin, gespikkelde rug en 'n wit gesig wat bruin raak op soek na kos in modderige water. Hulle plas in die water op soek na kos en duik soms om wiere en knolle te kry, maar eet ook graankorrels. Hulle staan regop met 'n uitgestrekte nek wanneer hulle angstig of ontsteld is. Die roep is 'n 'swee-swee-sweeu'-fluit.

LE CANARD A VISAGE BLANC (99)

Il a le cou long, noir à châtain, le dos brun tacheté. Le visage blanc est sale et brun quand il se nourrit dans les eaux boueuses. Le canard à visage blanc tripote pour la nourriture, et plonge quelquefois pour chercher des tubercules et de l'herbe dans l'eau. Il se nourrit aussi de grains. Cet oiseau très grégaire se tient debout, le cou étendu, quand il s'inquiète ou s'effraie. Le cri est un 'swee-swee-sweeu' caractéristique et sifflant.

WITWENENTE (99)

Kennzeichnend für den ausgewachsenen Vogel ist der lange, schwarz- bis kastanienbraune Hals, der braungebänderte Rücken und das weiße Gesicht, das durch die Futtersuche im Schlamm bräunlich-schmutzig sein kann. Diese Ente taucht nach Wasserpflanzen und -knollen, ernährt sich aber auch von Körnern. Sie lebt gesellig und steht mit aufrechtem Körper und emporgestrecktem Kopf da, wenn sie aufgeschreckt wird. Der Ruf ist ein pfeifender 'Wiii-Wiii-Wiiiuu'.

Dendrocygna viduata

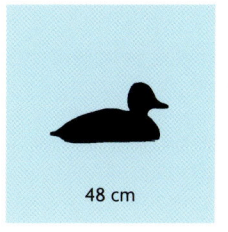

48 cm

Marakele,
Kruger,
Golden Gate Highlands,
Kalahari Gemsbok

Sagittarius serpentarius

SECRETARYBIRD (118)

This large, grey and black bird has extremely long legs, a bare yellow to red face and a hooked bill. Its name is derived from the long, quill-like nape feathers which are erected when it is alarmed or excited. Immatures have shorter central tail feathers than adults and a yellow face. They occur in savanna and grasslands, where they stride about on the ground, catching prey such as snakes or rodents.

SEKRETARISVOËL (118)

Dit is 'n groot grys-en-swart voël met uitermate lang bene, 'n kaal geel tot rooi gesig en 'n geboë snawel. Sy naam is afgelei van die lang, penveeragtige nekvere wat regop staan as die voël opgewonde is of geskrik het. Onvolwassenes lyk nes die volwassenes, maar het korter, sentrale stertvere en geel gesigte. Hulle kom voor in savanne en grasvelde waar hulle rondstap en slange of knaagdiere vang.

LE SECRETAIRE (118)

C'est un grand oiseau gris et noir aux pattes extrêmement longues, au visage jaune à rouge et au bec courbé. Son nom vient des longues plumes de la nuque ressemblant aux pennes qui se dressent quand il est effrayé ou excité. Les immatures ressemblent aux adultes mais les plumes centrales de la queue sont plus courtes et ils ont le visage jaune. Il se trouve à la savane et aux prairies, où il se promène à grands pas et attrape les serpents ou les rongeurs.

SEKRETÄR (118)

Dieser große Vogel hat außergewöhnlich lange Läufe, ein nacktes, gelb bis rötliches Gesicht und einen gekrümmten Schnabel. Der Name rührt von den aufstellbaren, federkielartigen Federn am Hinterkopf her. Jungvögel ähneln den Eltern, aber die mittleren Schwanzfedern sind kürzer, und das Gesicht ist gelb. Dieser Vogel kommt in Savanne und Grasfluren vor, wo er herumstelzt und Schlangen oder Nagetiere fängt und mitunter mit den Füßen zertritt.

Sagittarius serpentarius

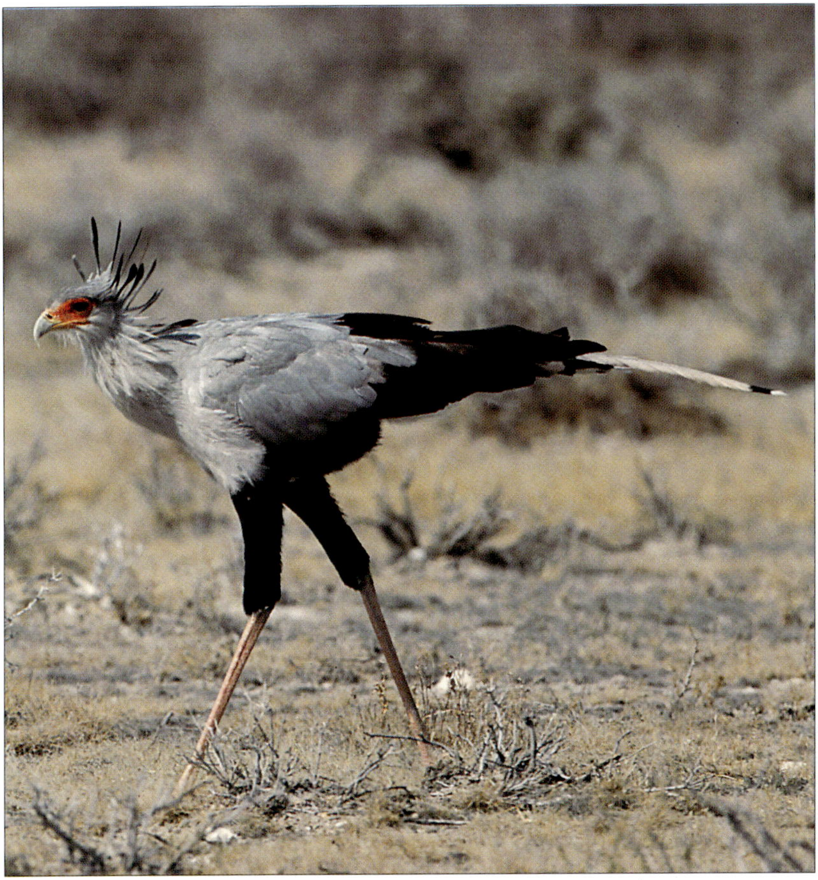

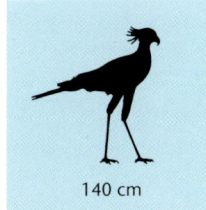

140 cm

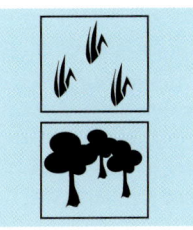

Addo Elephant, Bontebok,
Golden Gate Highlands,
Kalahari Gemsbok, Karoo,
Knysna National Lake Area,
Kruger, Marakele,
Tankwa Karoo, Mountain Zebra,
Tsitsikamma, Augrabies Falls,
\Hei-!Gariep, West Coast,
Wilderness

Gyps africanus

WHITEBACKED VULTURE (123)

The Whitebacked Vulture, one of Africa's commonest vultures, is often seen feeding at carcasses, where it makes loud hissing and cackling sounds as it fights for space with its kin and other vulture species. It has a dirty white colour, the white rump contrasting strongly with the rest of the dark upperparts. The nest is a flimsy stick structure situated at the top of a large tree.

WITRUGAASVOËL (123)

Die Witrugaasvoël, een van Afrika se bekendste aasvoëls, word dikwels gesien waar hy aan karkasse vreet en harde sis- en kekkelgeluide maak, al vegtende met lede van sy spesie asook ander aasvoëlspesies vir 'n spasie. Hulle het 'n vuilwit kleur; die wit romp steek skerp af teen die res van die bodele. Die nes, 'n tingerige struktuur van stokkies, word bo in 'n groot boom gebou.

LE VAUTOUR A DOS BLANC (123)

Très fréquent en Afrique, le vautour à dos blanc se rencontre souvent se nourrissant des carcasses, où il crie d'une voix sifflante et caquetante en se battant contre ses frères et contre d'autres vautours pour avoir une place. L'oiseau est blanc sombre, et le croupion blanc tranche sur le reste du corps supérieur. Le nid est une structure fragile de bâtons qui se trouve au sommet d'un grand arbre.

WEIßRÜCKENGEIER (123)

Der Weißrückengeier ist einer der häufigsten Geier in Afrika. Man sieht ihn oft an Kadavern fressen, wobei er laut vernehmliche, zischende und gackernde Laute ausstößt, während er sich mit seinen Artgenossen und anderen Geierarten um den Platz balgt. Er ist von schmutzigweißer Farbe, und der weiße Rücken hebt sich eindeutig von den dunkleren Flügeln ab. Das Nest ist eine lockere Struktur aus Stöcken im Gipfel eines großen Baumes.

Gyps africanus

95 cm

KALAHARI GEMSBOK,
\HEI-!GARIEP,
AUGRABIES FALLS,
MARAKELE,
KRUGER

Elanus caeruleus

BLACKSHOULDERED KITE (127)

This small, pointed-winged bird of prey is most often seen hovering with fast wing beats along roadsides and over fields, or perched on a prominent post, cocking its tail up and down, in search of food. Adults are grey with black shoulder patches, a silvery tail and a red eye. Immatures are browner with a yellowish eye. It is commonly found in association with agricultural lands.

BLOUVALK (127)

Hierdie klein roofvoël met sy gepunte vlerke word dikwels gesien waar hy langs die pad of oor landerye met vinnige vlerkslae fladder, of waar hy op 'n promi-nente plek sit, sy stert op en af wip en na kos soek. Volwassenes is grys met swart skouervlekke, 'n silwerige stert en 'n rooi oog. Onvolwassenes is bruiner met geler oë. Hierdie spesie word algemeen aangetref, veral naby landerye.

LE MILAN A L'EPAULE NOIRE (127)

Le milan à l'épaule noire est un petit oiseau de proie aux ailes pointues qui se voit le plus souvent se balançant en battant vite les ailes le long des bords de la route au-dessus des champs, cherchant la nourriture. Les adultes sont gris aux épaules tachées de noir, à la queue argentée et à l'oeil rouge. Les immatures sont plus bruns à l'oeil jaunâtre. Cette espèce se rencontre fréquemment, surtout près des champs agricoles.

GLEITAAR (127)

Diesen kleinen Greifvogel mit den spitz zulaufenden Flügeln sieht man häufig neben der Straße oder über den Feldern flatternd in der Luft verharren, oder er hockt auf einem Ausgucksposten und läßt seinen Schwanz auf- und nieder-schnellen. Der ausgewachsene Vogel ist grau mit schwarzen Schulterflecken, einem silbergrauen Schwanz und roten Augen. Jungvögel sind bräunlicher, mit gelblichen Augen. Dieser Vogel ist weit verbreitet, besonders auf Feldern.

Elanus caeruleus

33 cm

Addo Elephant, Bontebok,
Golden Gate Highlands,
Kalahari Gemsbok, Karoo,
Knysna National Lake Area,
Kruger, Marakele,
Tankwa Karoo, Mountain Zebra,
Tsitsikamma, Augrabies Falls,
\Hei-!Gariep, West Coast,
Wilderness

37

Circaetus gallicus

BLACKBREASTED SNAKE EAGLE (143)

This species is characterized by its naked, whitish legs. Adults have a yellow eye which contrasts with the black head, throat and upperparts. The lower body is white, flecked with black. Immatures are rusty brown in colour, have a light yellow eye, and a well-marked banded tail. In flight adults have an all-white underwing with black bands on the white flight feathers. They feed on snakes.

SWARTBORSSLANGAREND (143)

Hierdie spesie word gekenmerk aan sy kaal, witterige bene. Volwassenes het 'n geel oog wat afsteek teen die swart kop, keel en bodele. Die onderste dele is wit met swart vlekke. Onvolwassenes het 'n liggeel oog, roesbruin kleur en 'n duidelik gestreepte stert. In vlug vertoon volwassenes 'n wit ondervlerk met swart strepe op die wit primêre en sekondêre vere. Hulle jag in vlug.

L'AIGLE SERPENTEUR (143)

Les pattes blanches et nues typiques séparent cette espèce d'autres aigles aux pattes plumées. L'adulte a l'oeil jaune, la tête noire, le cou blanc et le corps supérieur tachetés de noir. Les immatures brun roux ont l'oeil jaune clair et la queue rayée bien marquée. Au vol, l'aile inférieure se montre toute blanche et le plumage de vol blanc est rayé de noir. Ils se nourrissent surtout de serpents et de lézards, et chassent au vol. Ils évitent les pays boisés.

SCHWARZBRUST-SCHLANGENADLER (143)

Charakteristisch für diesen Greifvogel sind die nackten, weißlichen Beine. Der ausgewachsene Vogel hat gelbe, vom schwarzen Kopf kontrastierende Augen, eine schwarze Kehle und einen schwarzen Rücken. Der untere Rumpf ist weiß mit schwarzen Flecken. Jungvögel sehen ähnlich aus. Das Flugbild zeigt weiße Unterflügeldecken mit schwarzgebänderten Arm- und Handschwingen. Sie ernähren sich vorwiegend von Eidechsen und Schlangen und jagen im Flug.

Circaetus gallicus

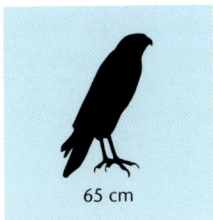

65 cm

Kruger, Kalahari Gemsbok,
\Hei-!Gariep, Augrabies Falls,
Marakele, Mountain Zebra,
Golden Gate, Karoo,
Marakele, Tankwa Karoo

Terathopius ecaudatus

BATELEUR (146)

This bird can easily be identified by its brightly coloured plumage, naked legs and very short tail. Its name in French implies an acrobat or tightrope walker, a reference to its in-flight action of rocking from side to side, rarely flapping its wings, as it glides about the sky. It feeds on snakes and leguaans, but may be seen scavenging at carcasses. It attains sexual maturity at eight years.

BERGHAAN (146)

Hierdie voël word gekenmerk aan sy helder vere, kaal bene en baie kort stert. Sy Franse naam beteken akrobaat of koordloper. Dit is afgelei van sy wiegbeweging in die lug wanneer hy sweef, en selde sy vlerke klap. Die Berghaan vreet slange en likkewane, maar word dikwels gesien waar hy aas by karkasse of diere wat doodgery is. Hierdie spesie bereik seksuele volwassenheid op 8 jaar.

LE BATELEUR (146)

Le plumage éclatant, les pattes nues et la queue très courte identifient très facilement cet oiseau. Son nom implique un acrobate ou un funambule, une allusion à son vol. Il se balance d'un côté à l'autre, en battant rarement les ailes, et en planant dans le ciel. Cette espèce se nourrit de serpents et de lézards. Il fouille dans les carcasses ou dans les mises à mort de la route. Il arrive à la maturité sexuelle à huit ans.

GAUKLER (146)

Dieser Vogel ist leicht an seinem farbenfreudigen Gefieder zu erkennen, den nackten Beinen und dem besonders kurzen Schwanz. Der französische Name, 'Bateleur', verweist auf einen Seiltänzer, ein Hinweis auf seine 'gaukelnde' Flugbewegung mit geringem Flügelschlag. Der Vogel ernährt sich von Schlangen und Warranen, man kann ihn aber auch oft am Straßenrand antreffen, wo er an Kadavern frißt. Der Gaukler ist mit acht Jahren geschlechtsreif.

Terathopius ecaudatus

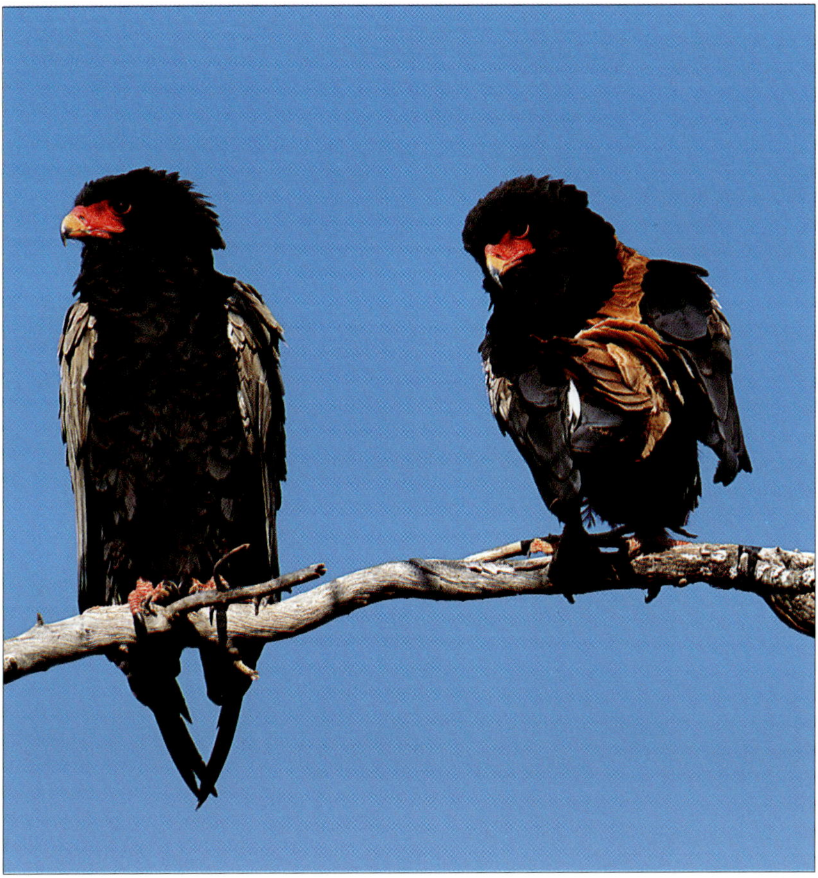

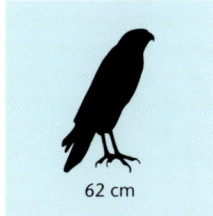

62 cm

Kruger,
Karoo,
Kalahari Gemsbok

Melierax canorus

PALE CHANTING GOSHAWK (162)

Frequently seen perched on telegraph poles along roadsides, this light grey-coloured bird of prey has a white rump and a light-coloured panel showing on the upperwing. It is found in the arid central and southwestern parts of the country, preferring thornveld habitat. The melodious, chanting call, 'kleeeu, kleeeu, klu klu klu', from which it takes its name, is repeated a number of times.

BLEEKSINGVALK (162)

Hierdie voël word dikwels gesien waar hy op telefoonpale langs paaie sit. Dit is 'n liggrys roofvoël met 'n wit romp en 'n ligkleurige strook op die vlerk. Hierdie spesie word aangetref in die droër sentrale en suidwestelike dele van die land en verkies doringveld as habitat. Die melodieuse, singende roep 'kleeeu-kleeeu-kloe-kloe-kloe' word 'n paar keer herhaal. Sy naam is afgelei van sy roep.

LE FAUCON CHANTEUR PALE (162)

Vu fréquemment perché sur un poteau télégraphique au bord des routes, le faucon chanteur pâle est un oiseau de proie gris au croupion blanc qui a une rayure claire à l'aile supérieure. Cette espèce se trouve dans les régions arides centrales et du sud-ouest du pays, préférant l'habitat épineux. Le cri monotone et mélodieux de cet oiseau, 'kleeeu, kleeeu, klu klu klu', d'où vient son nom, est répété plusieurs fois.

WEIßBÜRZEL-SINGHABICHT (162)

Man trifft diesen hellen, grauen Greifvogel ganz oft auf Telegrafenmasten am Straßenrand an; er hat einen weißen Bürzel, die Hinterkante der Armschwingen ist hell. Dieser Vogel kommt in den ariden Gebieten in der Mitte und im Süd-westen des Landes vor und bevorzugt Dornsavanne. Der klangvolle Flötenruf, 'Kliiiu-Kliiu-Klu-Klu-Klu-Klu-Klu', dem der Vogel seinen Namen verdankt, wird mehrmals wiederholt.

Melierax canorus

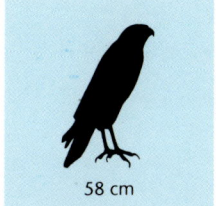

58 cm

RICHTERSVELD,
TANKWA KAROO,
AUGRABIES FALLS,
KALAHARI GEMSBOK,
\HEI-!GARIEP,
ADDO ELEPHANT,
MOUNTAIN ZEBRA,
KAROO,
MARAKELE

Falco tinnunculus

ROCK KESTREL (181)

This small falcon, which has rufous upperparts and underparts has a grey head streaked with black and a grey tail with a black terminal band. Females have narrow bands on the tail. The Rock Kestrel hunts from a perch or when hovering motionless in the sky. This species is commonly found on rocky ridges and mountainous terrain. The call is a shrill 'kee-kee-kee' or 'kik-kik-kik'.

KRANSVALK (181)

Hierdie klein valk wat rooibruin bo en onder is, het 'n grys kop met swart strepe en 'n grys stert met 'n swart buitelyn. Die Kransvalk jag van waar hy sit of vanuit die lug waar hy bewegingloos hang op soek na kos. Hierdie spesie word algemeen aangetref in bergagtige terrein en klipperige rante. Die roep is 'n skril 'kiee-kiee-kiee' of 'kiek-kiek-kiek'.

LA CRECERELLE DES ROCS (181)

Ce petit faucon roux a la tête striée de noir et la queue grise à une bande terminale noire. Les immatures sont plus pâles par endroits que les adultes. La crécerelle des rocs est un oiseau de proie qui chasse d'un perchoir ou en planant immobile dans le ciel en train de chercher la nourriture. Cette espèce se trouve généralement sur le terrain montagneux et sur les crêtes rocheuses. Le cri est un 'kee-kee-kee' ou 'kik-kik-kik' aigu.

TURMFALKE (181)

Dieser kleine Falke mit oben und unten rostfarbener Färbung hat einen grauen, schwarzgestreiften Kopf und einen grauen Schwanz mit dunkler Endbinde. Auf der Jagd hält sich der Turmfalke auf einem hochliegenden Sitzplatz auf, oder er schwebt im Rüttelflug auf der Stelle in der Luft. Er tritt meist in gebirgigem Gelände und an felsigen Steilhängen auf. Der Ruf ist ein hohes, schrilles 'Ki-Ki-Ki' oder 'Kik-Kik-Kik'.

Falco tinnunculus

36 cm

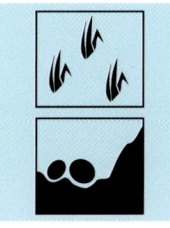

Addo Elephant, Bontebok, Golden Gate Highlands, Kalahari Gemsbok, Karoo, Knysna National Lake Area, Kruger, Marakele, Tankwa Karoo, Mountain Zebra, Richtersveld, Tsitsikamma, Augrabies Falls, \Hei-!Gariep, West Coast, Wilderness

Francolinus sephaena

CRESTED FRANCOLIN (189)

This white-streaked gamebird has a dark cap with a broad, white eye stripe, a dark bill and pinkish-red legs. The Crested Francolin is a common resident of dense riverine bush, bushveld and thick bush, especially near rocky hills. This species struts about on the ground, and may be seen running with its tail cocked. The call is a rattling 'chee-chakla, chee-chakla', repeated several times.

BOSPATRYS (189)

Hierdie witgestreepte wildvoël het 'n donker mus met 'n breë, wit oogstreep, 'n donker snawel en rooi bene. Die Bospatrys kom algemeen voor in bosveld, digte oewerplantegroei en digte bosse veral naby rotsagtige heuwels. Mannetjies pronk op die grond en hardloop dikwels met 'n opgeligte stert. Die roep is 'n kletterende 'tjee-tjakla, tjee-tjakla' wat verskeie kere herhaal word.

LE FRANCOLIN A CRETE (189)

Cet oiseau strié de blanc appartient au gibier à plumes. Le francolin à crête a le capuchon sombre, une rayure d'oeil large et blanche, le bec sombre et les pattes rouges. Cette espèce réside généralement dans la brousse épaisse des rivières, au bushveld, et dans la brousse épaisse surtout près des collines rocheuses. Il se pavane par terre et court la queue levée. Le cri aigu du francolin, 'chee-chakla, chee-chakla', est répété plusieurs fois.

SCHOPFFRANKOLIN (189)

Dieses weißgefleckte Federwild hat eine dunkle Kappe mit breiten, weißen Brauenstreifen; der Schnabel ist dunkel, die Beine sind rot. Der Schopffrankolin ist ein häufiger Bewohner des Flußdickichts, der Dornsavanne und des dichten Gestrüpps, besonders in der Nähe von felsigen Hügeln. Man kann ihn auf dem Boden herumstolzieren oder mit aufgerichtetem Schwanz flüchten sehen. Der Ruf ist ein schnarrendes, wiederholtes 'Tschii-Tschakla, Tschii-Tschakla'.

Francolinus sephaena

34 cm

KRUGER,
MARAKELE

Numida meleagris

HELMETED GUINEAFOWL (203)

This large gamebird has bluish facial skin, a bare head casque and a dark grey body flecked with white. It is a sociable species, often occurring in large groups. When disturbed it runs fast and flies off reluctantly. It roosts off the ground at night. During the day it forages on the ground in search of insects, fruits and berries. The contact call is a soft 'keet-keet-keet'.

GEWONE TARENTAAL (203)

Hierdie groot wildvoël het 'n blouerige gesigvel, 'n kaal helm en 'n donkergrys lyf met wit vlekke. Dit is 'n baie sosiale spesie en kom dikwels in groot groepe voor. Hulle hardloop vinnig wanneer hulle gehinder word. Hulle soek op die grond na insekte, vrugte en bessies, maar slaap nie snags op die grond nie. Die skrikroep is 'n sagte 'kieet-kieet-kieet'.

LA PINTADE A CASQUE (203)

Ce grand oiseau du gibier à plumes a la peau faciale bleuâtre, le casque de tête nu et le corps gris foncé tacheté de blanc. Une espèce sociétaire, elle se voit en grands groupes. Elle court vite quand on la dérange et s'envole à contrecoeur. Elle se juche au-dessus de la terre pendant la nuit et fouille par terre pour chercher des insectes et des fruits. Le cri de contact, 'keet-keet-keet', est typique de son habitat préféré, l'épine, la savane boisée et les terres agricoles.

PERLHUHN (203)

Dieses große Federwild hat eine bläuliche Gesichtshaut, einen nackten Scheitelaufsatz und einen dunklen, weißgesprenkelten, grauen Körper. Es tritt oft in großen Schwärmen auf. Das Perlhuhn kann schnell rennen, wenn es aufgestört wird, und hebt nur zögernd zum Flug ab. Nachts baumen die Vögel auf. Sie suchen am Boden nach Insekten, Früchten und Beeren. Der Ruf ist ein 'Kek-Kek-Kek-Kek', ein charakteristischer Laut in Dornsavanne und Feldern.

Numida meleagris

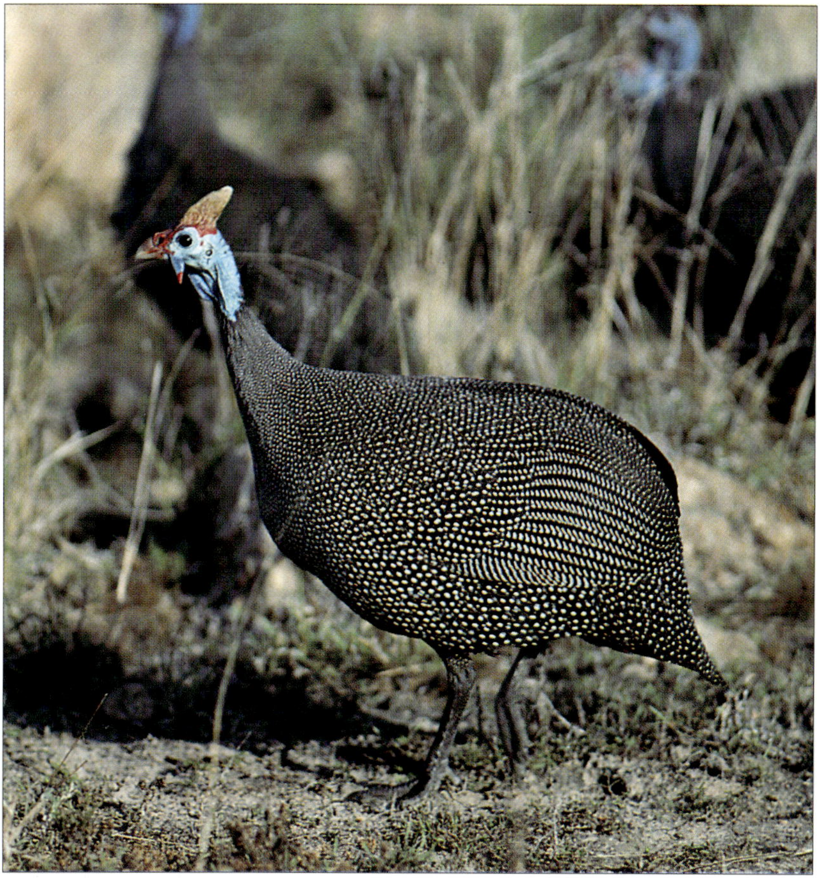

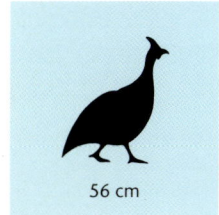

56 cm

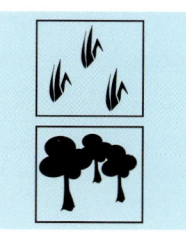

Addo Elephant,
Augrabies Falls, Bontebok,
Golden Gate, Kalahari Gemsbok,
Karoo, Knysna National Lake Area,
Kruger, Marakele, Mountain Zebra,
Tankwa Karoo, Tsitsikamma,
\Hei-!Gariep, West Coast, Wilderness

Anthropoides paradisea

BLUE CRANE (208)

The Blue Crane, South Africa's national bird, is threatened due to its diminishing habitat. This large, elegant bird is blue-grey in colour with a white crown, and long tail feathers which almost touch the ground. It occurs in Karoo scrub and grasslands, where it forages for seeds, grains, reptiles, frogs and insects. When not breeding, they may be found in large flocks of more than 50 individuals.

BLOUKRAANVOËL (208)

Die Bloukraanvoël word bedreig vanweë sy krimpende habitat. Hierdie groot, elegante voël is blougrys met 'n wit kroon en lang stertvere wat byna aan die grond raak. Hulle kom voor op grasvelde, in Karoostruikgewas waar hulle in die grond soek na saadjies, reptiele, paddas en insekte. Wanneer hulle nie broei nie, vorm hulle swerms van meer as 50 voëls. Die roep is 'n krakerige 'kraaank'.

LA GRUE DE PARADIS (208)

Ce grand oiseau bleu gris et élégant, au capuchon blanc, est l'oiseau national de l'Afrique du Sud. Les plumes de la queue touchent presque la terre. Il est menacé parce que son habitat diminue. Il se trouve dans les prairies, dans la brousse du Karoo et sur les terrains agricoles où il fouille pour trouver des graines, des reptiles, des grenouilles et des insectes. Quand il ne se reproduit pas, on le voit en grands troupeaux. Le cri, 'kraak', s'entend d'assez loin.

PARADIESKRANICH (208)

Der Paradieskranich, Südafrikas Nationalvogel, wird durch schwindendes Habitat bedroht. Dieser große, elegante, blaugraue Vogel hat einen weißen Scheitel und lange Schwanzfedern. Er kommt in der Karrulandschaft vor, Grasfluren und auf Feldern, wo er nach Samen, Körnern, Reptilien, Fröschen und Insekten sucht. Außerhalb der Brutzeit kann man große Schwärme antreffen. Der Ruf, ein hohes, kehliges 'Kräääk', ist weithin zu vernehmen.

Anthropoides paradisea

100 cm

BONTEBOK,
KAROO,
ADDO ELEPHANT,
MOUNTAIN ZEBRA,
GOLDEN GATE HIGHLANDS,
WILDERNESS

Gallinula chloropus

COMMON MOORHEN (226)

This is a common, sooty black waterbird with a red face shield, a yellow-tipped bill and yellow legs. Immatures are dark brown with a greenish face shield, bill and legs. On the water and when creeping about the edges of reedbeds, it flicks its tail up and down, showing a white undertail. It may be found on almost any stretch of open water where it forages for seeds, worms, insects and tadpoles.

GROOTWATERHOENDER (226)

Hierdie roetswart watervoël het 'n rooi frontale skild, 'n snawel met 'n geel punt en geel bene. Onvolwassenes is donkerbruin met 'n groenerige frontale skild en bene. Op die water en wanneer hulle in die riete rondkruip, beweeg die stert op en af, en vertoon 'n wit onderstert. Hulle word aangetref by enige oop stuk water waar hulle na saadjies, wurms, insekte en paddavissies soek.

LA GALLINULE COMMUNE (226)

C'est un oiseau de l'eau fréquent, noir, à masque facial rouge, à bout du bec et à pattes jaunes. Les immatures sont brun foncé à masque facial, à bec et à pattes verdâtres. A l'eau et en rampant aux bords des roselières, il dresse et baisse la queue inférieure blanche. On le trouve sur les étendues d'eau découvertes, entouré de roseaux et de prairies humides, où il fouille pour trouver des graines, des vers, des insectes et des têtards. Le cri est un 'krrruk' aigu.

TEICHHUHN (226)

Dieser häufige, pechschwarze Wasservogel hat eine rote Stirnplatte, eine gelbe Schnabelspitze und gelbe Beine. Jungvögel sind dunkelbraun, Stirnplatte, Beine und Schnabel grünlich. Auf dem Wasser und im Schilf wippt das Teichhuhn mit dem Schwanz und zeigt die weiße Unterschwanzdecke. Der Ruf ist ein scharfes 'Krrrik'. Man findet es an schilfumstandenen, offenen Gewässern und in feuchten Grasfluren, wo es nach Samen, Insekten und Kaulquappen sucht.

Gallinula chloropus

32 cm

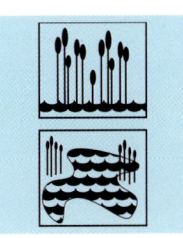

ADDO ELEPHANT, BONTEBOK,
GOLDEN GATE HIGHLANDS,
KALAHARI GEMSBOK, KAROO,
KNYSNA NATIONAL LAKE AREA,
KRUGER, MARAKELE, TANKWA KAROO,
MOUNTAIN ZEBRA, RICHTERSVELD,
TSITSIKAMMA, AUGRABIES FALLS,
\HEI-!GARIEP, WEST COAST,
WILDERNESS

Fulica cristata

REDKNOBBED COOT (228)

The Redknobbed Coot is black with a white face shield and bill, and two swollen red knobs on top of the forehead. Immatures are greyer and lack the red knobs. It is a common resident on open freshwater with some reeded vegetation. It spends much of its time on the water feeding on waterplants and grass, either by diving or from the surface. The call is a harsh 'kluk'.

BLESHOENDER (228)

Die Bleshoender is swart met 'n wit gesigskild en snawel en twee opgeswelde rooi knoppe bo-op die voorkop. Onvolwassenes is gryser en het nie hierdie rooi knoppe nie. Hierdie algemene standvoël kom voor in oop varswatergebiede met rietagtige plantegroei. Hulle spandeer baie tyd in die water waar hulle waterplante en -grasse vreet, deur óf af te duik óf op die oppervlak.

LA FOULQUE A BOSSES ROUGES (228)

Cet oiseau est noir, au masque facial et au bec blancs. Il a deux bosses rouges et enflées au front. Les immatures sont plus gris, sans les bosses. Elle habite généralement l'eau douce découverte à la végétation couverte de roseaux. Cette espèce reste sur l'eau ou plonge, se nourrissant de plantes aquatiques et d'herbe. Ces oiseaux agressifs se chassent souvent, et ils traversent l'eau à petits pas. Leur cri est un 'kluk' strident.

KAMMBLEßHUHN (228)

Das Kammbleßhuhn ist schwarz, Stirnplatte und Schnabel sind weiß, die zwei geschwollenen Kämme rot. Jungvögel sind grauer, es fehlen die Kämme. Das Kammbleßhuhn kommt häufig an Binnengewässern mit Schilfbestand vor. Es verbringt die meiste Zeit auf dem Wasser, wo es sich von Wasserpflanzen und Gras ernährt, sowohl stoßtauchend als auch auf der Oberfläche weidend. Die Vögel verhalten sich untereinander aggressiv. Der Ruf ist ein blechernes 'Klääck'.

Fulica cristata

44 cm

ADDO ELEPHANT, BONTEBOK,
GOLDEN GATE HIGHLANDS,
KALAHARI GEMSBOK, KAROO,
KNYSNA NATIONAL LAKE AREA,
KRUGER, MARAKELE, TANKWA KAROO,
MOUNTAIN ZEBRA, RICHTERSVELD,
TSITSIKAMMA, AUGRABIES FALLS,
\HEI-!GARIEP, WEST COAST,
WILDERNESS

Ardeotis kori

KORI BUSTARD (230)

The Kori Bustard, the largest bustard in the region, is reputed to be the world's heaviest flying bird. Likely to be seen only in our larger game reserves, this bird is unmistakable with its finely barred neck and breast and white belly. Males puff up their neck and breast feathers in display. They walk about with their bill angled upwards. They occur in dry grassland, thornveld and semidesert.

GOMPOU (230)

Die Gompou, die grootste pou in die streek, word beskou as die wêreld se swaarste voël wat vlieg. Hulle word net in ons groter wildreservate aangetref, en is onmiskenbaar met die fyn gestreepte nek en bors, en wit pens. Mannetjies blaas hulle nek- en borsvere op tydens pronkvertonings. Hulle loop met die snawel omhoog. Hulle kom op grasveld, doringveld en in semiwoestyn voor.

L'OUTARDE KORI (230)

La plus grande outarde de la région est peut-être l'oiseau volant le plus lourd du monde. On le trouve surtout dans nos plus grandes réserves nationales. Cette espèce est facile à reconnaître au cou délicatement rayé, et à la poitrine et le ventre blancs. Les mâles gonflent les plumes du cou et de la poitrine en paradant. Ces oiseaux se promènent le bec vers le haut aux prairies sèches, à l'épine et au semi-désert. Le cri retentissant et sonore est 'oom-oom-oom'.

RIESENTRAPPE (230)

Die größte Trappe dieses Gebietes soll auch der schwerste Flugvogel der Welt sein. Man trifft sie am ehesten in größeren Schutzgebieten an. Mit der fein-gesprenkelten Hals- und Brustpartie und dem weißen Bauch ist dieser Vogel unverkennbar. Diese Vögel stolzieren mit hochgerecktem Schnabel durchs Gelände und kommen in Dornsavanne, Graslandschaft und Halbwüste vor. Der Ruf ist ein tiefes, dröhnendes 'Uuum-Uuum'.

Ardeotis kori

135 cm

Kruger,
\Hei-!Gariep,
Mountain Zebra,
Karoo,
Tankwa Karoo,
Richtersveld,
Augrabies Falls,
Kalahari Gemsbok

Eupodotis afroides

NORTHERN BLACK KORHAAN (239b)

Males, with their orange to red bills and almost all-black underbodies and neck, are easily recognisable. Females are brown with a blackish belly and vent, but retain a pinkish base to the bill and yellow legs. Displaying males are noisy, calling a harsh 'kerrak-kerrak-kerrak-kerrack'. The display cruise ends with a slow descent with wings beating rapidly and legs dangling.

WITVLERKSWARTKORHAAN (239b)

Mannetjies word maklik uitgeken aan hulle oranje tot rooi snawels en meestal swart onderlyf en nek. Wyfies is bruin met 'n swarterige pens en kloaak, en het geel bene en 'n pienkerige snawelbasis. Pronkende mannetjies is raserig en roep skel 'kerrak-kerrak-kerrak-kerrak'. Die vertoning eindig met 'n stadige landing, terwyl vlerke vinnig klap en bene rondswaai.

LE TETRAS LYRE NOIR DU NORD (239b)

Les mâles, au bec orangé à rouge, au sous-corps et au cou presque tout à fait noirs, sont facilement reconnaissables. Les femelles sont brunes à ventre noirâtre, à base du bec rosée et à pattes jaunes. Les mâles bruyants qui paradent crient 'kerrak-kerrak-kerrak-kerrack' au vol et par terre. A la fin de la parade, ils descendent lentement, en battant rapidement les ailes, les pattes ballantes. Ils fouillent par terre pour trouver des insectes et de la matière végétale.

GACKELTRAPPE (239b)

Männchen sind an ihren orangeroten Schnäbeln und nahezu gänzlich schwarzer Unterseite und Halspartie leicht zu erkennen. Weibchen sind braun, unten und an der Kloake schwarz, und an Schnabelwurzel und Ansatz der gelben Läufe rosa. Balzende Männchen lärmen mit schnarrendem 'Karrak-Karrak' im Flug und auf dem Boden. Das Flugspiel beendet der langsame Landeflug mit Geschwirr und baumelnden Beinen. Diese Vögel suchen am Boden nach Insekten.

Eupodotis afroides

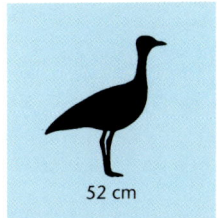

52 cm

Richtersveld,
Augrabies Falls,
Kalahari Gemsbok,
Karoo,
\Hei-!Gariep,
Golden Gate Highlands,
Marakele,
Mountain Zebra

Actophilornis africanus

AFRICAN JACANA (240)

This bird is also known as the 'Lily-trotter', as it has very long toes enabling it to walk on waterlily leaves without sinking. Adults are rufous-brown with a white throat, and a light blue forehead and bill. Males incubate the eggs and look after the youngsters. It feeds on crustaceans and insects, foraged from floating vegetation. This noisy bird makes a grating 'krrrek-krrrek' sound.

GROOTLANGTOON (240)

Hierdie voël het lang tone wat hom in staat stel om op waterlelieblare te loop sonder om te sink. Volwassenes is roesbruin met 'n wit keel, 'n ligblou voorkop en snawel. Onvolwassenes is valer as volwassenes. Die mannetjie broei die eiers uit en pas die kleintjies op. Hulle vreet skaaldiere en insekte wat hulle uit die drywende plantegroei kry. Die roep is 'n krapperige 'krrrek-krrrek'-geluid.

LE JACANA AFRICAIN (240)

On l'appelle le trotteur de lis, parce que ses très longs doigts de patte le permettent de marcher sur les nénuphars sans couler. Les adultes brun roux à la gorge blanche ont le front et le bec bleu. Les immatures sont plus ternes. Les mâles couvent les oeufs. Cette espèce se trouve aux lagunes, aux marécages et aux bords des bras de décharge à la végétation émergente. Ils se nourrissent de crustacés et d'insectes. Le cri bruyant et grinçant est 'krrrek-krrrek'.

JACANA (240)

Seine überlangen Zehen ermöglichen es dem Vogel, auf Wasserpflanzen zu laufen. Ausgewachsene Vögel sind rostbraun mit weißer Kehle; Stirnplatte und Schnabel sind hellblau. Jungvögel sind unscheinbarer. Männchen brüten die Eier aus und kümmern sich um die Küken. Man trifft diese Spezies an Lagunen, Teichen und Flußauen an. Die Vögel leben von Krustentierchen und Insekten. Der Ruf ist ein lärmendes, schnarrendes 'Krrrääk-Krrrääk'.

Actophilornis africanus

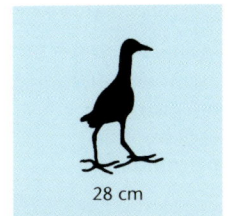

28 cm

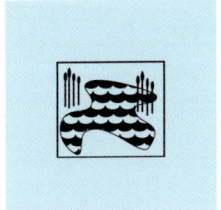

KRUGER,
KALAHARI GEMSBOK

Charadrius tricollaris

THREEBANDED PLOVER (249)

This small shorebird has a distinctive bright red eye ring, a red base to the bill and two broad black breast bands. It occurs throughout the region along sandy shorelines on inland lakes, coastal estuaries and river sandbanks. It runs in short spurts, pecks at the sand with short jabs and flies away with jerky wing beats. The call is a high-pitched, piping 'peep-peep-peep', uttered in flight.

DRIEBANDSTRANDKIEWIET (249)

Hierdie klein strandvoël het 'n kenmerkende helderrooi oogring, twee breë borsbande en 'n rooi snawelbasis. Hulle kom al langs die sanderige oewers van binnelandse mere, kusmondings en riviersandbanke voor. Hulle hardloop kort entjies, pik na die sand met kort steekbewegings en vlieg met 'n rukkerige vlerkgeklap op. Hierdie spesie kom regoor Suid-Afrika voor.

LE PLUVIER A TROIS RAYURES (249)

Ce petit oiseau de la côte à cerne rouge vif, à base du bec rouge et à deux larges rayures de poitrine se trouve presque partout en Afrique du Sud le long des rivages sablonneux des lacs intérieurs, aux estuaires côtières et aux bancs de sable des rivières. Il court aux efforts soudains, picote au sable et vole en battant les ailes d'une manière saccadée. Le cri est un 'peep-peep-peep' aigu et sifflant, poussé en volant.

DREIBANDREGENPFEIFER (249)

Dieser kleine Küstenvogel hat einen auffallenden, roten Augenring, eine rote Schnabelwurzel und eine breite Doppelbänderung an der Brust. Er kommt in der gesamten Region vor, an den sandigen Ufern von Seen, an Ästuarien und auf Sandbänken in Flüssen. Er rennt ruckartig, pickt mit abgehackten Bewegungen im Sand und fliegt mit ruckartigem Flügelschlag. Sein Ruf ist ein helles, durchdringendes Pfeifen, 'Wiet-Wiet-Wiet', im Flug.

Charadrius tricollaris

18 cm

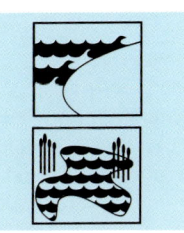

Addo Elephant, Bontebok,
Golden Gate Highlands,
Kalahari Gemsbok, Karoo,
Knysna National Lake Area,
Kruger, Marakele, Tankwa Karoo,
Mountain Zebra, Richtersveld,
Tsitsikamma, Augrabies Falls,
\Hei-!Gariep, West Coast,
Wilderness

Vanellus coronatus

CROWNED PLOVER (255)

These brown birds have long, red legs, a black crown surrounded by a white ring, and a white belly. Immatures are similar to adults but duller, with yellow legs and a yellow base to the bill. Crowned Plovers can be seen in large flocks out of breeding season, feeding on insects. They are noisy birds, making a scolding 'kreeep-kreeep-kreeep' sound.

KROONKIEWIET (255)

Hierdie bruin voël het lang, rooi bene, 'n swart kroon wat omring word deur 'n wit ring, en 'n wit pens. Onvolwassenes lyk dieselfde, maar is dowwer en het geel bene en 'n geel snawelbasis. Kroonkiewiete verkies kort grasvelde. Hulle kom in groot swerms voor na die broeityd, terwyl hulle op soek is na insekte. Hulle is luidrugtig en maak 'n kras 'krieeep-krieeep-krieeep'-geluid.

LE PLUVIER COURONNE (255)

Ils sont bruns aux pattes longues et rouges, au ventre blanc, et à la couronne noire entourée de blanc. Les immatures moins vifs ont les pattes et la base du bec jaunes. Cette espèce préfère les prairies, les champs d'aviation et les terrains de sport, et se voit au bord des autoroutes et des refuges gazonnés. Hors de la saison de reproduction, ils se nourrissent en grands troupeaux d'insectes. Ils font du bruit et poussent un cri grondeur 'kreeep-kreeep-kreeep'.

KRONENKIEBITZ (255)

Diese braunen Vögel haben lange, zinnoberrote Beine, einen weißen Bauch und eine schwarze Kappe, die von einem weißen Ring umgeben ist. Jungvögel sind ähnlich, aber unscheinbarer, mit gelben Beinen und gelbem Schnabelansatz. Sie bevorzugen trockenes Grasland, Flughäfen und Sportfelder; sind aber auch am Straßenrand und auf Verkehrsinseln anzutreffen. Außerhalb der Nistzeit sieht man sie in großen Schwärmen. Sie stoßen ein scheltendes 'Kriiep-Kriiep' aus.

Vanellus coronatus

30 cm

Addo Elephant, Bontebok,
Golden Gate Highlands,
Kalahari Gemsbok, Karoo,
Knysna National Lake Area,
Kruger, Marakéle, Tankwa Karoo,
Mountain Zebra, Richtersveld,
Tsitsikamma, Augrabies Falls,
\Hei-!Gariep, West Coast,
Wilderness

Vanellus armatus

BLACKSMITH PLOVER (258)

The Blacksmith Plover's name is derived from its call, 'klink, klink, klink', which sounds like an anvil being hammered. This black, white and grey shorebird is found in association with dams, pans and wetlands. Immatures are brown where the adults are black. It feeds on insects and worms. They are most often seen in pairs, although they may gather in larger numbers when not breeding.

BONTKIEWIET (258)

Die Engelse naam van hierdie spesie is afgelei van sy roep wat klink soos 'n smid wat besig is om op 'n aambeeld te hamer – 'klink, klink, klink'. Onvolwassenes is bruin, terwyl volwassenes swart is. Hierdie swart, wit en grys oewervoël word naby watergebiede aangetref. Hulle vreet insekte en wurms, en word meestal in pare gesien. Die Bontkiewiet maak eerste alarm wanneer hy 'n indringer gewaar.

LE PLUVIER FORGERON (258)

Son cri, 'klink, klink, klink', ressemble au son d'une enclume en train d'être martelée. Cet oiseau côtier noir, blanc et gris se trouve près des réservoirs, des bassins et des pays humides. Les immatures sont bruns, les adultes noirs. Il se nourrit d'insectes et de vers. Ils se voient le plus souvent par couples, mais ils se réunissent en grand nombre quand ils ne se reproduisent pas. Cet oiseau bruyant est le premier à donner l'alerte en voyant un importun.

WAFFENKIEBITZ (258)

Dieser schwarzweiß und graugemusterte Küstenvogel wird an Stauseen, Salzpfannen und Marschgebieten angetroffen. Der Name bezieht sich auf seinen Ruf, 'Tink, Tink, Tink', der wie der Hammerschlag auf einem Amboß klingt. Jungvögel sind braunweiß. Der Vogel ernährt sich von Insekten und Würmern. Meist lebt er paarweise, aber außerhalb der Nistzeit versammeln sich große Schwärme. Sein lärmender Ruf warnt vor Eindringlingen.

Vanellus armatus

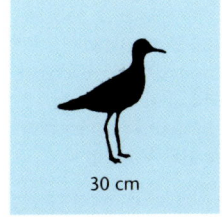

30 cm

Addo Elephant, Bontebok,
Golden Gate Highlands,
Kalahari Gemsbok, Karoo,
Knysna National Lake Area,
Kruger, Marakele, Tankwa Karoo,
Mountain Zebra, Richtersveld,
Tsitsikamma, Augrabies Falls,
\Hei-!Gariep, West Coast,
Wilderness

Recurvirostra avosetta

AVOCET (294)

A large black and white shorebird, the Avocet has a distinctive fine, long, upturned bill. It occurs on estuaries, flooded pans and inland lagoons. This species feeds on worms, small fish and insects by sweeping its bill from side to side through the water. Highly nomadic, these birds are often seen in large flocks of more than 100 individuals, flying in 'V' formations.

BONTELSIE (294)

Hierdie groot, swart-en-wit oewervoël het 'n fyn, smal, snawel wat boontoe buig. Hulle kom voor by oorstroomde panne, binnelandse strandmere en mondings. Hulle vreet wurms, klein vissies en insekte deur die snawel van die een kant na die ander kant deur die water te trek. Hulle is nomadies en swerms van meer as 'n 100 voëls vlieg dikwels in V-formasie.

L'AVOCETTE (294)

C'est un grand oiseau côtier noir et blanc, facile à reconnaître, l'avocette a le bec étroit, fin, et retroussé. On peut le voir aux estuaires, aux bassins inondés et aux lagunes. Cette espèce se nourrit de vers, de petit poissons et d'insectes en tournant rapidement le bec dans l'eau. Très nomades, ces oiseaux se voient souvent en grands troupeaux de plus de 100 oiseaux, volant en formations 'V'. Le cri est un 'kooit' clair.

SÄBELSCHNÄBLER (294)

Der Säbelschnäbler ist ein großer, schwarzweißer Küstenvogel mit einem bezeichnenden, dünnen, nach oben gebogenen Schnabel. Man trifft diese Vogel gewöhnlich an Ästuarien, überschwemmten Salzpfannen und Lagunen an. Er ernährt sich gründelnd von Würmern, kleinen Fischen und Insekten und ist ein nomadischer Vogel. Oft sieht man große Schwärme von über 100 Vögeln in einer V-Formation fliegen.

Recurvirostra avosetta

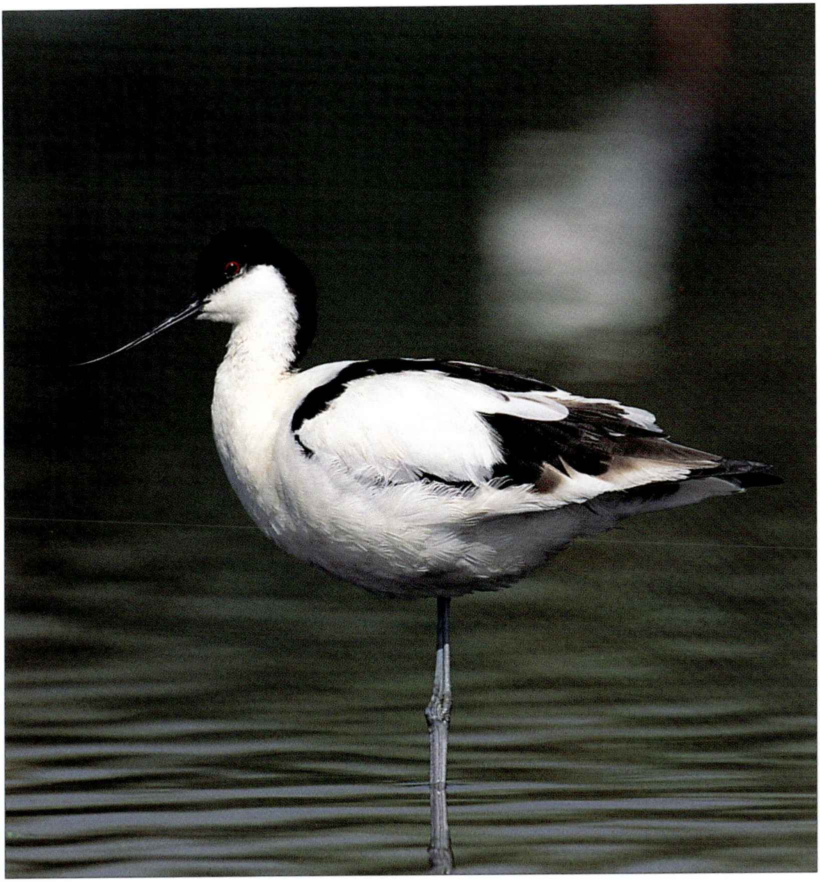

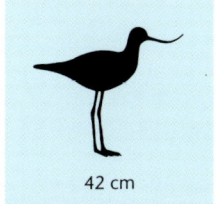

42 cm

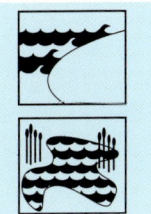

West Coast,
Tankwa Karoo,
Kalahari Gemsbok,
\Hei-!Gariep, Bontebok,
Karoo, Mountain Zebra,
Addo Elephant,
Wilderness, Kruger,
Knysna National Lakes Area

Smutsornis africanus

DOUBLEBANDED COURSER (301)

This small, plover-like bird has very long, white legs, a short, stumpy decurved bill, a brown back, wings with buffy edges, and two distinct, broad breast bands. A bird of semidesert areas, this species prefers stony gravel plains with little grass. This highly nomadic species occurs solitarily or in pairs. The call is a thin, whistled 'peeeu-wee', dropping in pitch before rising again.

DUBBELBANDDRAWWERTJIE (301)

Hierdie klein, kiewietagtige voël het baie lang, wit bene, 'n kort, stomp snawel, 'n bruin rug en vlerke met dofgeel rande sowel as twee kenmerkende breë borsbande. Hoewel hulle in semiwoestyngebiede aangetref word, verkies hulle klipperige gruisvlaktes met min gras. Hierdie nomadiese spesie kom alleen voor of in pare. Hulle roep is 'n yl 'tieeo-wee'-fluit wat styg en daal in toon.

LE COURVITE A DEUX RAYURES (301)

Cette espèce très nomade des régions du semi-désert qui ressemble au pluvier a de très longues pattes blanches, le petit bec court et trapu, le dos brun, les bouts d'ailes jaunes, et deux larges raies de poitrine. Le courvite à deux rayures préfère les plaines de gravier rocailleux où il y a peu d'herbe. Ce petit oiseau se rencontre seul ou par couples. Le cri est un 'peeeu-wee' fluette et sifflé, qui baisse avant de remonter.

DOPPELBANDRENNVOGEL (301)

Dieser kleine, kiebitzartige Vogel hat lange, weiße Beine und einen kurzen, gedrungenen Schnabel, Rücken und Flügel sind braun mit helleren Rändern, und er weist zwei charakteristische, breite Bruststreifen auf. Als Bewohner der Halbwüste bevorzugt er Kiesebenen mit spärlichem Graswuchs. Diese eindeutig nomadische Spezies tritt einzeln oder paarweise auf. Der Ruf ist ein schwaches, pfeifendes 'Tiiu-Wie', mit fallender und ansteigender Tonlage.

Smutsornis africanus

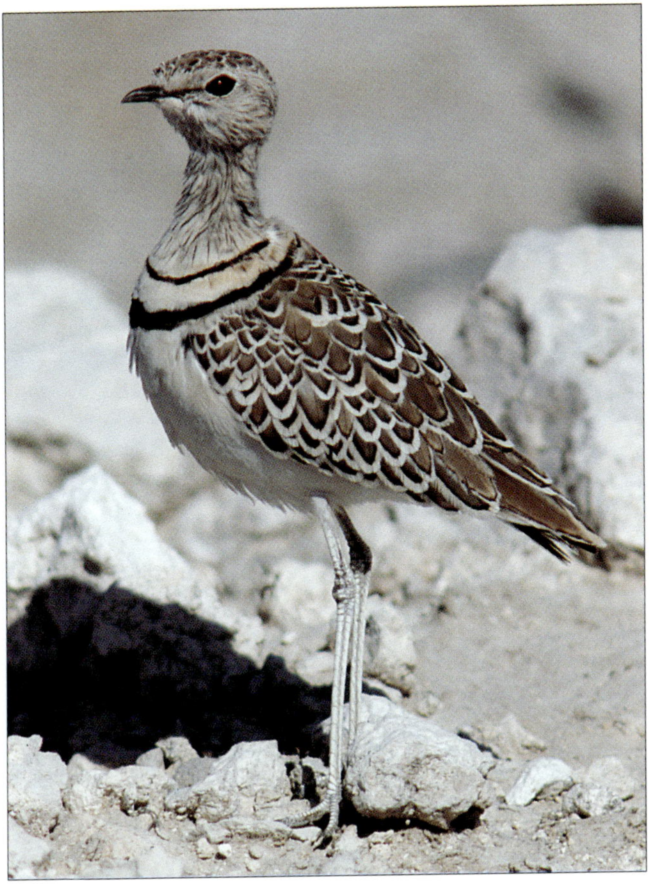

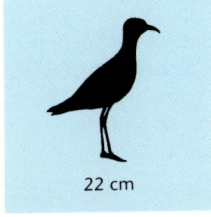

22 cm

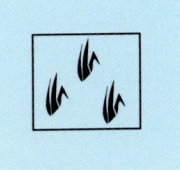

Richtersveld,
Augrabies Falls,
Kalahari Gemsbok,
\Hei-!Gariep,
Tankwa Karoo,
Karoo,
Mountain Zebra

Larus dominicanus

KELP GULL (312)

The Kelp Gull, our largest resident gull, is a coastal species and most common on the West Coast. Both adults and immatures are white with a black back and wings, a large yellow bill and greenish legs. These birds occur in harbours, estuaries and along open coasts, where they forage for fish, offal, birds' eggs and chicks. The call is a screaming 'meeeu'.

SWARTRUGMEEU (312)

Die Swartrugmeeu, ons grootste standvoël, is 'n kusspesie en kom algemeen voor aan die Weskus. Volwasse en onvolwasse voëls is wit met 'n swart rug en swart vlerke, 'n groot, geel snawel en groenerige bene. Hierdie voëls kom voor in hawens, mondings en langs die kus, waar hulle na vis, afval, die eiers van voëls en kuikens soek. Die roep is 'n skreeuende 'meeeu'.

LA MOUETTE VARECH (312)

Notre plus grande mouette résidante, la mouette varech est un oiseau côtière, et c'est la mouette la plus fréquente de l'ouest. Les adultes et les immatures sont blancs au dos et aux ailes noirs, au grand bec jaune et aux pattes verdâtres. On la trouve aux ports, aux estuaires et le long de côtes découvertes, fouillant pour trouver du poisson, des déchets, des oeufs d'oiseau et des poissons. Le cri de cet oiseau est un 'meeeu' perçant.

DOMINIKANERMÖWE (312)

Die Dominikanermöwe, die größte einheimische Möwe, ist ein Küstenvogel und kommt besonders häufig an der Westküste vor. Ausgewachsene und junge Vögel sind weiß, Rücken und Handschwingen schwarz, der große Schnabel ist gelb, die Beine sind grünlich. Diese Vögel kommen oft in Häfen vor, an Ästuarien und an der offenen Küste, wo sie sich von Fisch, Eingeweiden, Vogeleiern und Vogeljungen ernähren. Der Ruf ist ein kreischendes 'Miii-ork'.

Larus dominicanus

60 cm

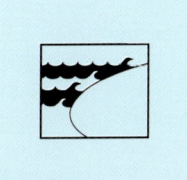

West Coast,
Wilderness,
Knysna National Lakes Area,
Tsitsikamma

Streptopelia capicola

CAPE TURTLE DOVE (354)

The grey-coloured Cape Turtle Dove with its black collar or ring on the hindneck is one of the commonest doves in the region. This species can be found in virtually any habitat other than forest. It feeds mostly on insects and seeds. It breeds throughout the year, hence its abundance. The call is well known in Africa, sounding like 'work-harder'.

GEWONE TORTELDUIF (354)

Hierdie gryskleurige tortelduif met sy swart kraag of ring agterop die nek is een van die algemeenste duiwe in die streek. Hierdie spesie word in feitlik enige habitat aangetref, behalwe in woude. Hulle vreet meestal insekte en sade. Hulle broei dwarsdeur die jaar – daarom is hulle so volop. Die roep is baie bekend in Afrika en klink soos die Engelse woorde 'work harder'.

LA TOURTERELLE DES BOIS DU CAP (354)

Au col ou au cercle noir derrière le cou, cet oiseau est une des tourterelles les plus fréquentes et répandues de la région. On trouve la tourterelle des bois du Cap presque partout au pays sauf dans les forêts. Elle se nourrit surtout d'insectes et de graines. Cette espèce se reproduit toute l'année, de là son abondance. Le cri de cet oiseau est bien connu en Afrique, et semble dire les mots anglais 'work-harder'.

KAPTURTELTAUBE (354)

Die graugefiederte Kapturteltaube mit ihrem schwarzen Nackenband zählt zu den häufigsten Tauben dieses Gebiets. Im Flug zeigt sie ihren weißrandigen Schwanz und die weiße Schwanzspitze. Diese Vögel kann man fast überall, außer im Wald, antreffen. Sie ernähren sich hauptsächlich von Insekten und Samen. Die Vögel brüten das ganze Jahr hindurch, daher sind sie so zahlreich. Der Dreiklang ihres Rufes ist in Afrika wohlbekannt.

Streptopelia capicola

28 cm

Addo Elephant, Bontebok,
Golden Gate Highlands,
Kalahari Gemsbok, Karoo,
Knysna National Lake Area,
Kruger, Marakele, Tankwa Karoo,
Mountain Zebra, Richtersveld,
Tsitsikamma, Augrabies Falls,
\Hei-!Gariep, West Coast,
Wilderness

Corythaixoides concolor

GREY LOURIE (373)

This large, all-grey bird has a long tail and a prominent head crest which can be raised and lowered at will. This species occurs in thornveld, wooded savanna, riverine habitat and suburbia. This agile bird runs up and down trees and leaps clumsily from branch to branch. A fruit feeder, it also eats buds, leaves and insects. The noisy Grey Lourie utters a harsh, nasal 'ga-waaaay' sound.

KWÊVOËL (373)

Hierdie groot, grys voël het 'n lang stert en 'n prominente kuif wat na willekeur regop kan staan en plat kan lê. Kwêvoëls kom in doringveld, beboste savanne, en in die omgewing van riviere voor. Hulle is rats voëls wat op en af in die bome rondhardloop en lomp van tak tot tak spring. Hulle is vrugtevreters, maar vreet ook blomknoppe, blare en insekte. Hulle uiter 'n harde, nasale 'gawaaay' geluid.

LE TOURACO GRIS (373)

Gris, à longue queue, il a une huppe prononcée, qu'il dresse et baisse à volonté. Cette espèce se trouve à l'épine, à la savane boisée, près des rivières, et dans la banlieue. Agile, il monte et descend les arbres en courant et saute maladroitement de branche en branche. Il se nourrit de fruits, de bourgeons, de feuilles et d'insectes. Bruyant, il pousse un cri rauque et nasal, 'ga-waaaay', ou 'go-away', 'va-t'en' en français, d'où son autre nom, 'l'oiseau va-t'en'.

GRAULÄRMVOGEL (373)

Dieser große, reingraue Vogel hat einen langen Schwanz und eine auffällige Haube, die nach Bedarf aufgestellt oder angelegt wird. Man trifft ihn in der Dornsavanne, der Baumsavanne, in Galeriewäldern und Vorortgärten an. Äußerst behende läuft er an Baumstämmen hinauf und herunter und hüpft schwerfällig von Ast zu Ast. Er lebt von Früchten, auch von Knospen, Blättern und Insekten und stößt ein rauhes, nasales 'Koo-Wäi' aus.

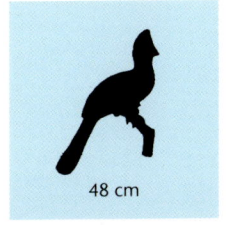

48 cm

Kruger,
Marakele

Cuculus solitarius

REDCHESTED CUCKOO (377)

The loud male call, 'weet-weet-weeoo', often translated as 'Piet-my-vrou', is distinctive of this bird. It is a large, grey cuckoo with a red chest and a barred belly. This bird lays its eggs in the nests of a range of species, including robins, chats and thrushes. It feeds on insects, preferring caterpillars. A summer visitor to the region, it occurs in forests and heavy woodlands.

PIET-MY-VROU (377)

Die luide, kenmerkende roep van die mannetjie, 'weeet-weet-weeoo' word vertolk as 'Piet-my vrou'. Dit is 'n groot, grys koekoek met 'n rooi bors en gestreepte pens. Wyfies lê hulle eiers in die neste van verskeie voëls onder andere janfrederikke en lysters. Hulle vreet insekte, maar verkies ruspes. Hulle besoek die streek in die somer en kom voor in woude en digte boswêreld.

LE COUCOU A COU ROUGE (377)

Le cri retentissant du mâle, 'weet-weet-weeoo', est le signe distinctif de ce grand coucou gris à poitrine rouge et à ventre strié, qui pond ses oeufs dans les nids d'autres espèces, comme les rouges-gorges, les tariers et les grives. Il se nourrit d'insectes, préférant les chenilles. Un visiteur d'été, il se trouve dans les forêts, dans les bois épais, aux parcs et dans les jardins. Il y a quelques tribus locales qui croient que son retour annonce l'arrivée du printemps.

EINSIEDLERKUCKUCK (377)

Es ist ein großer, grauer Kuckuck mit rotbrauner Brust und gestreiftem Bauch. Der laute Ruf des Männchens, ein 'Wiiet-Wiiet-Wiiuu' oder 'Piet-my-vrou', ist charakteristisch für diesen Vogel. Der Vogel legt seine Eier in verschiedene Nester, darunter die von Rotkehlchen, Schmätzern und Drosseln. Er ernährt sich von Insekten, vorzugsweise Raupen. Als Sommergast der Region trifft man ihn in Wäldern, dichten Baumhainen, Parks und Gärten an.

Cuculus solitarius

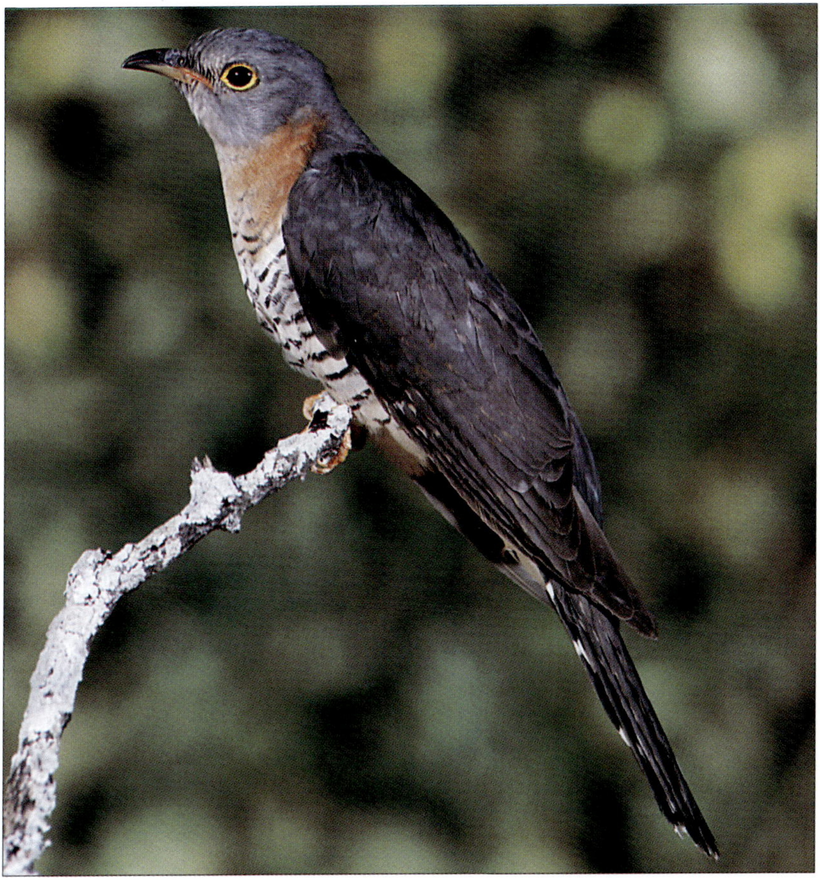

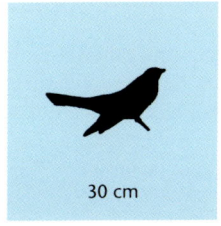

30 cm

West Coast,
Bontebok, Wilderness,
Knysna National Lakes Area,
Tsitsikamma,
Addo Elephant,
Mountain Zebra,
\Hei-!gariep,
Marakele, Kruger,
Golden Gate Highlands

Centropus burchelli

BURCHELL'S COUCAL (391a)

This black and white bird with its russet wings has a red eye and a stout, slightly decurved bill. This species forages in vegetation, and on the ground where it feeds on nestling birds, frogs, large crickets and small mammals. It can be found skulking in dense thickets, woodlands, reedbeds and suburban gardens. The call is a liquid 'glug-glug-glug', sounding like water emptying from a bottle.

GEWONE VLEILOERIE (391a)

Hierdie swart-en-wit voël met sy rooibruin vlerke het 'n rooi oog en 'n effens geboë snawel. Gewone Vleiloeries soek kos in plantegroei en op die grond, waar hy voëls wat nes maak, vreet; hulle vreet ook paddas, groot krieke en klein soogdiere. Hulle skuil in digte struikgewasse. Die roep is 'n borrelende 'glug-glug-glug' wat klink soos water wat uit 'n bottel vloei.

LE COUCAL DE BURCHELL (391a)

Cette espèce noire et blanche aux ailes rousses, à l'oeil rouge et au gros bec décourbé fouille dans la végétation et par terre pour se nourrir d'oisillons, de grenouilles, de grands grillons et de petits mammifères. On trouve le coucal de Burchell caché dans les bosquets épais, aux bois, aux roselières et dans les jardins de la banlieue. Le cri harmonieux et gai, 'glug-glug-glug', a le son de l'eau qui coule d'une bouteille.

TIPUTIP (391a)

Dieser schwarzweiße Vogel hat rostbraune Flügeln, rote Augen und einen kräftigen, leicht gebogenen Schnabel. Die Spezies sucht unter Pflanzen und auf dem Boden nach Nahrung, wo sie sich von Nestlingen, Fröschen, großen Grillen und kleinen Säugetieren ernährt. Sie schleicht im Dickicht, in Waldgebieten, im Schilf und in Vorortgärten umher. Der gurgelnde Ruf, 'Glug-glug-glug', klingt wie aus einer Flasche rinnendes Wasser.

Centropus burchelli

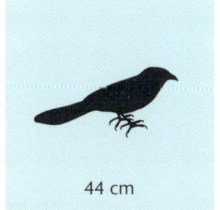

44 cm

Knysna National Lakes Area,
Kruger,
Marakele,
Bontebok,
Tsitsikamma,
Wilderness,
Addo Elephant

Glaucidium perlatum

PEARLSPOTTED OWL (398)

This species, our smallest owlet, has yellow eyes and two black 'eye spots' at the back of the head, but lacks ear tufts. Despite its size, it feeds aggressively on insects, mice and small birds. Normally crepuscular, it may be seen sitting on telegraph poles during daylight hours. Songbirds often mob it if it attracts attention during the day by calling; the call is a series of 'pheeu, pheeu' notes.

WITKOLUIL (398)

Die Witkoluil, ons kleinste uiltjie, het geel oë en twee swart 'valsoë' agter sy kop, maar nie oorklosse nie. Ten spyte van sy grootte vreet hy baie insekte, muise en kleiner voëls. Hoewel hulle tydens skemer gesien word, word hulle ook gedurende die dag aangetref waar hulle op telefoonpale sit. Hulle word dikwels nageboots deur sangvoëls. Die roep is 'n reeks 'peeeu, peeeu'-note.

LA CHOUETTE TACHETE DE PERLES (398)

Le plus petit de nos hiboux a les yeux jaunes et deux 'taches d'oeil' noires derrière la tête. Elle se nourrit d'une manière agressive d'insectes, de souris et de petits oiseaux. Crépusculaire, elle se trouve à l'épine et aux pays boisés à larges feuilles. On la voit assise sur les poteaux télégraphiques pendant la journée. Cet hibou est souvent attaqué par les oiseaux chanteurs s'il attire leur attention en criant; le cri, 'pheeu, pheeu', est une série de notes qui montent et descendent.

PERLKAUZ (398)

Der kleine Perlkauz hat gelbe Augen und zwei schwarze Nackenflecken, aber keine Federohren. Er verzehrt gierig Insekten, Mäuse und kleine Vögel. Obgleich diese Vögel Dämmerungstiere sind, kann man sie auch am Tage auf Telegrafenmasten sitzen sehen, besonders im Winter. Der Ruf besteht aus einer Reihe steigender und fallender Pfeiftöne, 'Fiu-Fiu-Fiu'. Man trifft den Kauz in der Dornsavanne und in breitblättrigem Waldland an.

Glaucidium perlatum

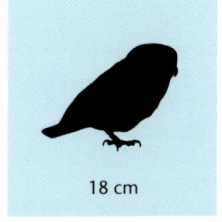

18 cm

Kruger,
Marakele,
Kalahari Gemsbok,
Augrabies Falls,
\Hei-!Gariep

Bubo africanus

SPOTTED EAGLE OWL (401)

The bright yellow eyes, ear tufts on top of the head and the hooting 'hu-hooo' call are good identification features of this bird. Our commonest owl, this resident species has adapted very well to the urban environment where it is frequently seen perched on telegraph poles, keeping a tight control on the urban rodent population. This bird can be found throughout southern Africa.

GEVLEKTE OORUIL (401)

Die heldergeel oë, oorklosse op die kop en die 'hoe-hoee'-roep is die uitstaande kenmerke van hierdie uil. Hierdie standvoël, ons algemeenste uil, het goed by die stedelike omgewing aangepas waar hy dikwels op telefoonpale sit. Hulle beheer ook die stedelike knaagdierbevolking. Gevlekte Ooruile word dwarsdeur suidelike Afrika aangetref in ligbeboste savannegebiede en oop grasvelde.

LE GRAND-DUC TACHETE (401)

Les yeux jaunes, les touffes d'oreilles sur la tête et le cri ululant, 'hu-hooo', identifient cet oiseau. Notre hibou le plus fréquent, cette espèce résidante s'est très bien adaptée à l'environnement urbain où l'oiseau se voit souvent perché sur les poteaux télégraphiques, contenant très bien la population de rongeurs. Il se trouve partout en Afrique du Sud à la savane légèrement boisée, aux pays couverts de forêts épaisses et aux pays découverts sans arbres.

FLECKENUHU (BERGUHU) (401)

An den leuchtend gelben Augen, den Federohren and dem typischen 'Hu-Huuuh' ist dieser Vogel leicht zu bestimmen. Als häufigste einheimische Eule, hat sie sich der städtischen Umgebung gut angepaßt, wo man sie häufig auf Telegrafenmasten hocken sieht; sie hält die städischen Nagetiere im Schach. Diesen Vogel trifft man im gesamten südlichen Afrika an, in lichter Baumsavanne, dichten Laubwäldern und baumloser, offener Grassteppe.

Bubo africanus

47 cm

Addo Elephant, Bontebok,
Golden Gate Highlands,
Kalahari Gemsbok, Karoo,
Knysna National Lake Area,
Kruger, Marakele, Tankwa Karoo,
Mountain Zebra, Richtersveld,
Tsitsikamma, Augrabies Falls,
\Hei-!Gariep, West Coast,
Wilderness

Colius striatus

SPECKLED MOUSEBIRD (424)

The Speckled Mousebird with its elongated and untidy tail belongs to one of the few bird families specific to Africa. The blackish legs and black and white bill separate it from the other mousebirds. They are clumsy fliers appearing to crash into bushes on landing. They may be seen scrambling about in fruiting trees, feeding at peculiar angles on wild berries, new buds, fresh leaves and fruit.

GEVLEKTE MUISVOËL (424)

Die Gevlekte Muisvoël met sy verlengde en slordige stert behoort aan een van die min voëlfamilies wat endemies is aan Afrika. Die swart-en-wit snawel en swarterige bene onderskei hom van ander muisvoëls. Hulle kan gesien word waar hulle in vrugtebome rondskarrel, op soek na wilde bessies, nuwe bloeisels, vars blare en gekweekte vrugte. Hulle is lomp vlieërs.

L'OISEAU-SOURIS TACHETE (424)

D'une famille rare spécifique à l'Afrique, il a la queue allongée et ébouriffée. Les pattes noirâtres et le bec blanc le séparent d'autres oiseaux-souris. Cette espèce se voit se bousculant dans les arbres fructifères, se nourrissant, en biais bizarres, de baies, de bourgeons, de feuilles vertes et de fruits cultivés. Ce sont des aviateurs maladroits et semblent emboutir des arbustes en atterrissant. On les trouve dans les régions plus humides du sud et de l'est de l'Afrique australe.

BRAUNFLÜGELMAUSVOGEL (424)

Der Braunflügelmausvogel mit seinem langen, unordentlichen Schwanz gehört zu den wenigen Vogelfamilien, die nur in Afrika vorkommen. Die schwärzlichen Beine und der schwarzweiße Schnabel unterscheiden diesen Vogel von anderen Mausvögeln. Er lebt von wilden Beeren, frischen Knospen, zarten Blättchen und Obst. Diese Vögel sind ungeschickt im Fliegen. Ihre Verbreitung beschränkt sich auf die feuchteren Gebiete im Süden und Osten Südafrikas.

Colius striatus

35 cm

BONTEBOK,
TSITSIKAMMA,
WILDERNESS,
KNYSNA NATIONAL LAKES AREA,
ADDO ELEPHANT,
MOUNTAIN ZEBRA,
GOLDEN GATE HIGHLANDS,
KRUGER, MARAKELE

Ceryle rudis

PIED KINGFISHER (428)

This species, the only black and white kingfisher in the region, is a common resident and an expert fisher. Males have two black breast bands and females a single one. It is confined to larger inland, slow-moving rivers, dams and coastal estuaries. The call is a high-pitched chatter, uttered as it fishes on the wing, hovering with fast-beating wings and maintaining its head pointed downwards.

BONTVISVANGER (428)

Die Bontvisvanger, die enigste swart-en-wit visvanger in die streek, is 'n vaardige visvanger en 'n algemene standvoël. Mannetjies het twee swart borsbande, terwyl wyfies net een het. Hulle is beperk tot die groter binnelandse, stadig vloeiende riviere en damme. Die roep is 'n hoë geklets, wat geuiter word terwyl hulle vanuit die lug visvang met vinnig klappende vlerke en die kop onderstebo.

L'ALCYON PIE (428)

Le seul martin-pêcheur de la région est répandu et un pêcheur expert. Les mâles ont deux rayures de poitrine noires et les femelles en ont une. Il se borne aux plus grandes rivières de l'intérieur qui se meuvent lentement, aux estuaires côtières, aux lagunes et aux barrages. Le cri est un caquetage aigu, poussé pendant qu'il pêche au vol, se balançant en battant rapidement les ailes, la tête immobile et dirigée vers la terre.

GRAUFISCHER (428)

Der Graufischer ist der einzige Eisvogel mit schwarzweißem Gefieder. Er ist häufig und ein vorzüglicher Fischer. Das Männchen hat zwei schwarze Brust-streifen und das Weibchen nur einen. Der Ruf ist ein hohes Gezwitscher, das ausgestoßen wird, während er rüttelnd, mit unbewegtem Kopf und abwärts gerichtetem Schnabel über der Wasserfläche verharrt. Er lebt nur an größeren, träge fließenden Flüssen, Küstenästuarien, Lagunen und Stauseen.

Ceryle rudis

28 cm

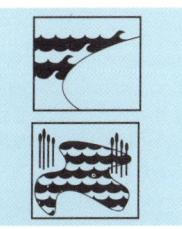

Kruger, Marakele,
Golden Gate Highlands,
\Hei-!Gariep, Karoo,
Mountain Zebra,
Addo Elephant, Tsitiskamma,
Knysna National Lakes Area,
Wilderness, Bontebok,
West Coast, Augrabies Falls,
Tankwa Karoo, Richtersveld

Alcedo cristata

MALACHITE KINGFISHER (431)

This small but colourful kingfisher has an iridescent red bill, blue upperparts, and rufous cheeks and underparts. It inhabits quiet backwaters, riverine habitat, larger rivers with well-developed reedbeds, and riverbanks in which it breeds. Perching near the water on a reed or a stick, it dives head first into the water and brings its prey back to the perch, and then stuns and swallows it whole.

KUIFKOPVISVANGER (431)

Hierdie klein, kleurvolle visvanger het 'n reënboogkleurige rooi snawel, blou bolyf, en rooibruin wange en onderlyf. Hulle bewoon stil opdamwater, rivieragtige habitat en strome waar hulle broei. Hierdie spesie sit gewoonlik naby die water op 'n riet of tak, duik dan kop eerste in die water en bring die prooi terug na waar hy gesit het; hy slaan sy prooi katswink en sluk dit dan heel in.

LE MARTIN-PECHEUR MALACHITE (431)

Petit et coloré, il a le bec rouge iridescent, le corps supérieur bleu, le corps inférieur et les joues roux. Il habite aux roselières mûres, près des rivières et aux bras de décharge tranquilles, et se reproduit sur leurs rives. Se perchant près de l'eau sur un roseau ou sur un bâton, il plonge, la tête la première, dans l'eau, et ramène sa proie au perchoir, l'assomme et l'avale sans la mâcher. Cette espèce est très territoriale et habite partout dans la région.

MALACHITEISVOGEL (431)

Dieser kleine, farbenfreudige Vogel hat einen schillernden roten Schnabel. Er ist oben blau, unten und an den Wangen rotbraun. Er lebt an ruhigen, abgelegenen Gewässern, in Auen, an Bächen und größeren Flüssen mit Schilfbeständen, wo er am Ufer nistet. Der Malachiteisvogel hockt in der Nähe des Wassers auf einem Schilfhalm oder Zweig, erhascht stoßtauchend seine Beute und kehrt auf seinen Platz zurück. Dieser Vogel verteidigt sein Wohn- und Nahrungsgebiet.

Alcedo cristata

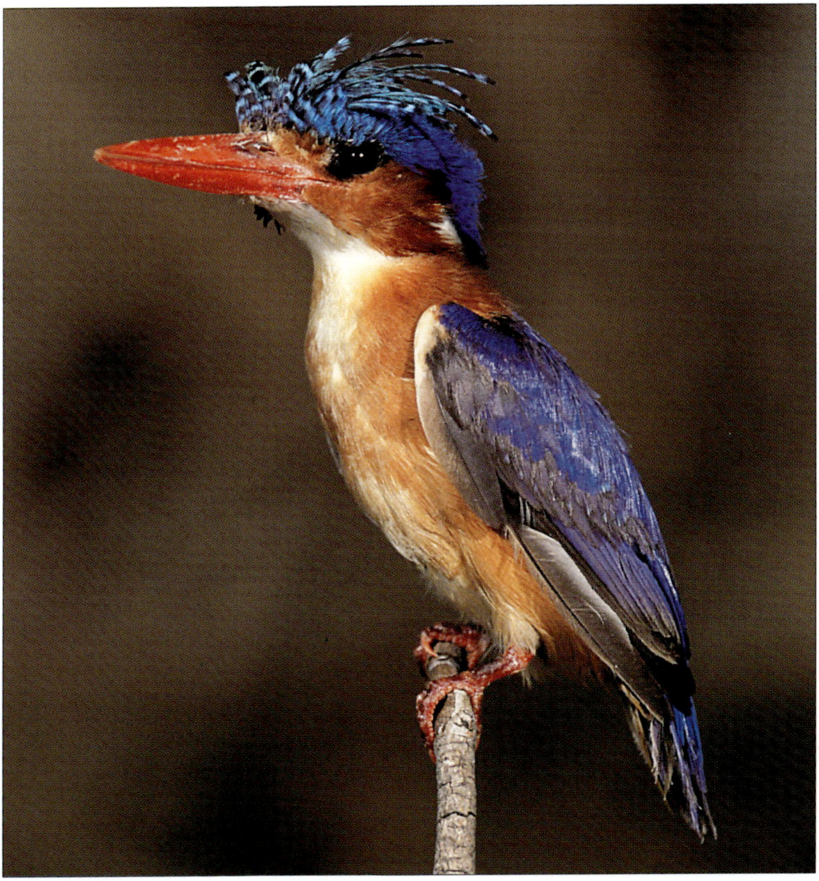

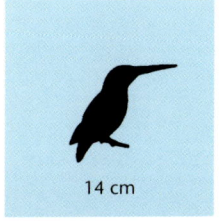

14 cm

Richtersveld,
Augrabies Falls,
\Hei-!Gariep, West Coast,
Bontebok, Tsitsikamma,
Knysna National Lakes Area,
Wilderness, Addo Elephant,
Golden Gate Highlands,
Kruger, Marakele,
Mountain Zebra

Merops pusillus

LITTLE BEE-EATER (444)

The green and yellow Little Bee-eater, our smallest bee-eater, has a square yellow tail with a black band near the tip, and a yellow throat with a black breast band. It may be seen in woodland, forest margins and on the edges of thickets, where the sharp 'chip-chip' call often gives away its presence. This bird sallies from a perch of a twig or grass stem, returning to eat its prey.

KLEINBYVRETER (444)

Die geel-en-groen Kleinbyvreter, ons kleinste byvreter, het 'n vierkantige, geel stert met 'n swart band naby die punt, en 'n geel keel met 'n swart borsband. Hulle word aangetref in bosgebiede en op die rante van struikgewasse waar hulle 'n skerp 'tjip-tjip'-geluid maak. Hierdie voël vlieg van waar hy sit op 'n tak of grasspriet net om weer daarnatoe terug te keer om sy prooi te vreet.

LE PETIT GUEPIER (444)

Vert et jaune, notre plus petit guêpier a la queue jaune et carrée, une rayure noire près du bout, la gorge jaune à rayure noire de poitrine. On le voit dans le pays boisé, aux lisières des forêts et aux bords des bosquets, où le cri aigu 'chip-chip' révèle souvent sa présence. Il quitte un perchoir de brindelle ou de tige d'herbe, rentrant seulement pour manger sa proie; il utilise souvent le même perchoir jour après jour.

ZWERGBIENENFRESSER (444)

Der grüngelbe Zwergbienenfresser, der kleinste Bienenfresser des Gebiets, hat einen geradeabgeschnittenen, gelben Schwanz mit schwarzer Endbinde, eine gelbe Kehle mit schwarzem Brustband. Man sieht den Vogel im Wald, am Waldrand und am Rande vom Dickicht, wo sein helles 'Tschipp-Tschipp' seine Anwesenheit verrät. Er stößt von seinem Zweig oder Grashalm herab und kehrt dann zurück, um seine Beute dort zu verzehren.

Merops pusillus

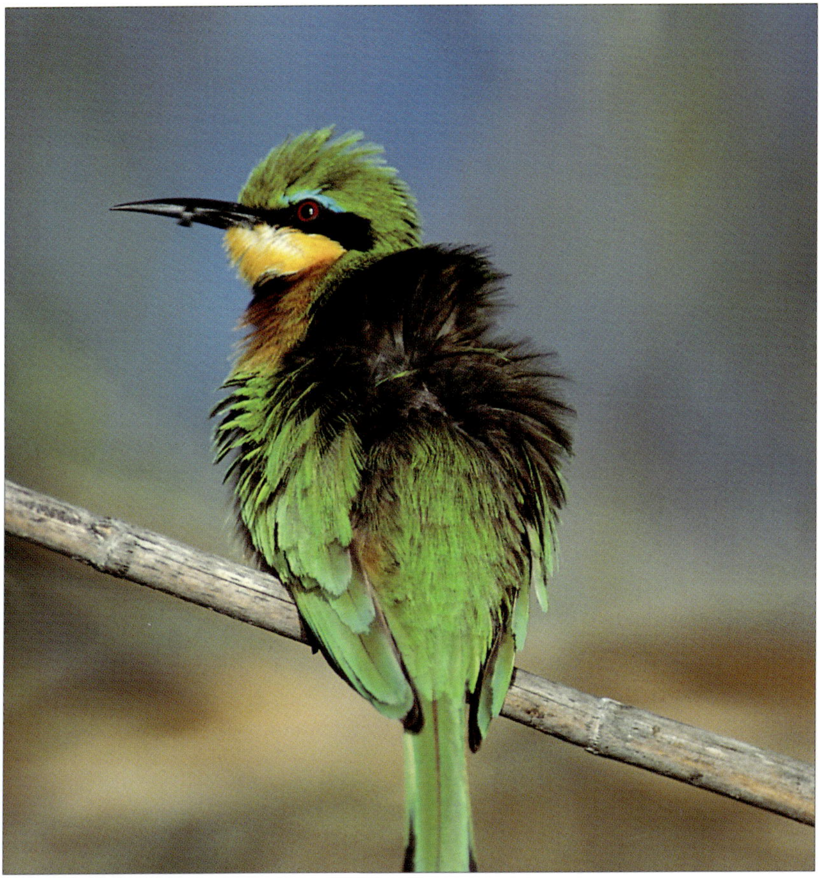

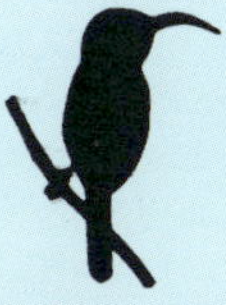

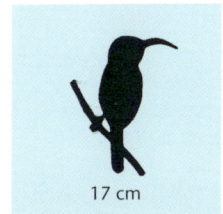

17 cm

Kruger,
Marakele

Coracias naevia

PURPLE ROLLER (449)

This unmistakable bird has a heavy white eyebrow, a brownish-green crown and back, and lilac-brown underparts heavily streaked with white. The Purple Roller, the largest and least noisy roller in our region, perches in one place for long periods of time. During its rock-and-roll display flight, it calls 'chik-kaaa, chik-kaaa, kakakaka'. It is most often seen alone in thornveld and in open woodland.

GROOTTROUPANT (449)

Die onmiskenbare Groottroupant het 'n swaar, wit wenkbrou, 'n bruinerige groen kroon en rug, en persbruin onderste dele wat swaar wit gestreep is. Die Groottroupant, die grootste en stilste troupant in ons streek, sit vir lang periodes op een plek. Gedurende sy ruk-en-rol vlugvertoning roep hy 'karaa-karaa'. Hulle word dikwels alleen in doringveld aangetref, asook in oop bosgebiede.

LE PIGEON CULBUTANT (449)

Cet oiseau facilement reconnaissable a le sourcil blanc et gros, la couronne et le dos vert brunâtre, et le sous-corps brun lilas fortement strié de blanc. C'est le plus grand pigeon et le moins bruyant de notre région. Il se perche longtemps dans un seul endroit. Au vol de parade rock-and-roll, cette espèce crie 'chik-kaaa, chik-kaaa, kakakaka'. D'habitude c'est un habitant de l'épine et du pays découvert, où il se voit seul.

STRICHELRACKE (449)

Diese unverkennbare Racke hat breite weiße Augenstriche, einen bräunlich-grünen Scheitel und Rücken und eine weißgestrichelte, lilabraune Unterseite. Die Strichelracke, die größte und am wenigsten lärmende Racke des Gebiets verharrt für lange Zeit auf der gleichen Stelle. Während des Rock-and-Roll-Flugspiels stößt der Vogel ein rauhes 'Tschik-kaa, Tschik-kaa' aus. Man trifft ihn meist einzeln in der Dornsavanne an; gewöhnlich ist er an ein Revier gebunden.

Coracias naevia

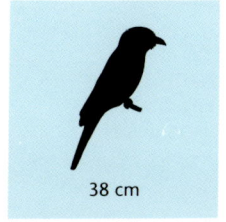

38 cm

Kruger,
Marakele,
Kalahari Gemsbok

Upupa africana

HOOPOE (451)

An unmistakable cinnamon-coloured bird, the Hoopoe has an erectile, black-edged crest which it raises when alarmed. Its flight – short, shallow wing beats interspersed with glides – shows an obvious black and white wing pattern. This common resident probes with its long, decurved bill in the ground in search of crickets or insect larvae. The call is a 'hoop-hoop-hoop' or 'hoop-hoop'.

HOEPHOEP (451)

Hierdie onmiskenbare kaneelkleurige voël het 'n swartpuntkuif wat hy oopsprei wanneer hy skrik. In vlug, 'n kort, vlak vlerkgeklap onderbreek deur sweef-bewegings, is sy duidelike swart-en-wit vlerkpatroon sigbaar. Hierdie standvoël kom algemeen in oop bosgebiede en doringveld voor, waar hy met sy lang, afgeboë snawel na insekte op die grond soek. Mannetjies roep 'hoep-hoep-hoep'.

LA HUPPE (451)

Cet oiseau a une huppe érectile au bout noir qu'il dresse quand il s'alarme. Son vol se rappelle celui d'un grand papillon, et laisse voir un dessin d'aile noir et blanc très frappant. Cet habitant fréquent des jardins, des pays découverts et de l'épine se nourrit par terre, fouillant de son long bec décourbé pour trouver des grillons, des larves d'insectes et des lombrics. Les mâles crient quelquefois sans cesse leur 'hoop-hoop-hoop' ou 'hoop-hoop' caractéristique.

WIEDEHOPF (451)

Ein unverwechselbarer, zimtfarbener Vogel. Der Wiedehopf hat einen aufstellbaren, schwarzrandigen Federschopf. Seine Flugbewegung erinnert an einen Schmetterling und zeigt die scharzweiße Flügelzeichnung. Er lebt in Gärten, Dornsavanne und Laubwäldern und sucht auf dem Boden nach Nahrung. Die Männchen lassen mitunter anhaltend ihr charakteristisches 'Huuup-Huuup-Huuup' ertönen.

Upupa africana

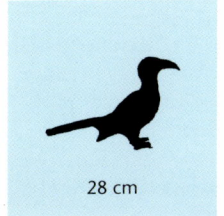

28 cm

Addo Elephant, Bontebok,
Golden Gate Highlands,
Kalahari Gemsbok, Karoo,
Knysna National Lake Area,
Kruger, Marakele, Tankwa Karoo,
Mountain Zebra, Richtersveld,
Tsitsikamma, Augrabies Falls,
\Hei-!gariep, West Coast,
Wilderness

Tockus flavirostris

SOUTHERN YELLOWBILLED HORNBILL (459)

This species' red throat patch, deep yellow eye surrounded by bare red skin, and large, yellow bill separate it from any other hornbill in the area. An omnivore, foraging mostly on the ground where ground cover is sparse, this bird eats termites, grasshoppers, caterpillars, seeds and berries. The call, a characteristic sound of the bushveld, is a rapid 'kok-kok-koka-koka-koka'.

GEELBEKNEUSHORINGVOËL (459)

Hierdie spesie se diepgeel oog wat omring word deur 'n kaal, rooi vel, sy rooi keelkol en die groot, geel snawel onderskei hom van ander neushoringvoëls in die gebied. Dit is 'n wydverspreide standvoël. Hulle is omnivore en soek meestal kos, soos termiete, sprinkane, ruspes, sade en bessies, op die grond waar die grondbedekking min is. Die roep is 'n vinnige 'kok-kok-kok-koka-koka'.

LE TOCK DU SUD A BEC JAUNE (459)

L'oeil jaune enfoncé de cette espèce, entouré de peau nue rouge, la tache de gorge rouge et le grand bec jaune la séparent d'autres tocks de la région. C'est un habitant universel de l'épine et des pays boisés à larges feuilles et plus secs. Omnivore, fouillant surtout par terre où le pays est presque découvert, il se nourrit de graines, de baies, et d'insectes. Le cri, un son typique de la brousse, est un 'kok-kok-kok-koka-koka-koka' rapide.

GELBSCHNABELTOKO (459)

Das kräftig gelbe Auge, umgeben von nackter roter Haut, der rote Kehlfleck und der große, gelbe Schnabel unterscheiden ihn von anderen Tokos in dem Gebiet. Er ist in der Dornsavanne und den trockeneren, breitblättrigen Laubwäldern weit verbreitet. Er ist ein Allesfresser und sucht meistens auf dem Boden nach Termiten, Heuschrecken und anderen Insekten, sowie Raupen, Samen und Beeren. Der Ruf ist ein kennzeichnendes 'Kock-Kock-Kock-Kocka-Kocka-Kocka'.

Tockus flavirostris

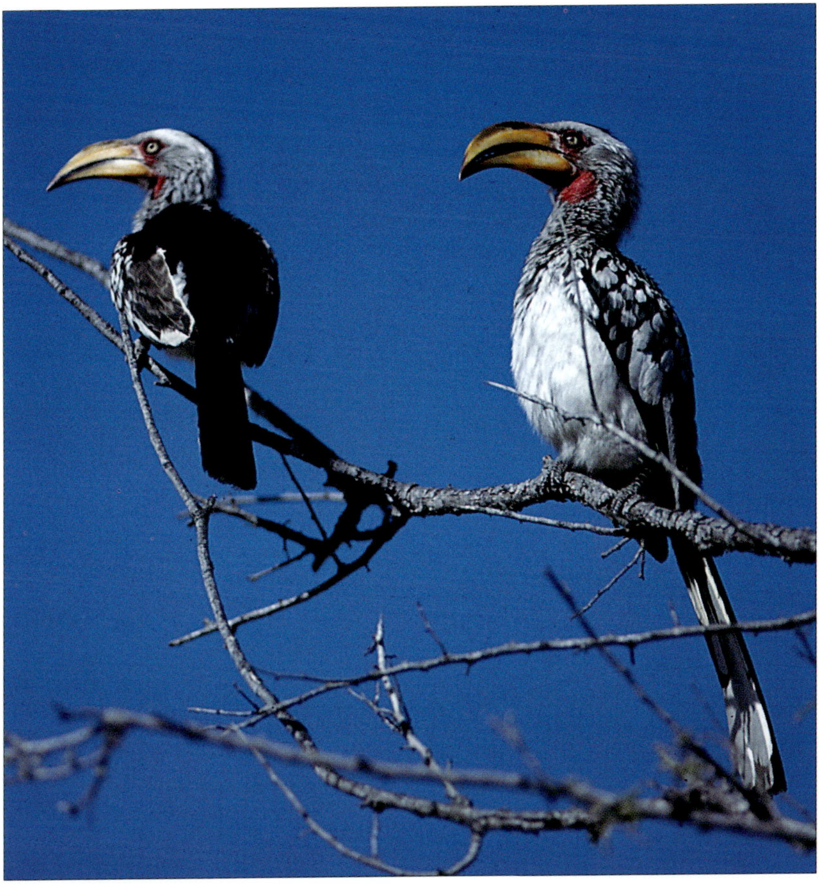

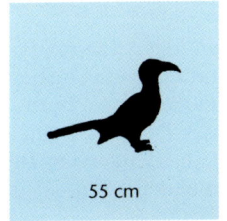

55 cm

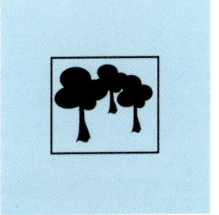

Kruger,
Marakele,
Kalahari Gemsbok

Bucorvus leadbeateri

GROUND HORNBILL (463)

This large, black, turkey-sized bird has a heavy decurved bill and a red throat and eye patch. Immatures resemble the adult but have a yellowish throat and eye patch. An aberrant hornbill, being predominantly terrestrial, this species digs on the ground with its bill for reptiles, frogs, insects and small mammals. Its deep booming call, 'du-du-dududu', is often heard in the early morning.

BROMVOËL (463)

Hierdie groot, swart voël, wat so groot soos 'n kalkoen is, het 'n rooi oogkol en 'n swaar, afgeboë snawel. Onvolwassenes het 'n gelerige keel en oogkol. Bromvoëls is hoofsaaklik grondbewonend. Hulle krap in die grond met hulle snawel en soek na reptiele, paddas, insekte en klein soogdiere. Hulle diep, dreunende 'doe-doe-doedoeee' kan dikwels in die vroeë oggend gehoor word.

LE CALAO TERRESTRE (463)

Cet oiseau noir, de la taille d'un dinde, a le bec lourd décourbé et des taches d'oeil rouges. Les immatures ont la gorge et les taches d'oeil jaunâtres. Un calao aberrant, étant surtout terrestre, cette espèce fouille du bec par terre pour trouver des reptiles, des grenouilles, des insectes et de petits mammifères. Son cri profond et résonant, 'du-du-dududu', s'entend souvent de grand matin. La superstition la protège dans quelques régions.

HORNRABE (463)

Dieser putengroße, schwarze Vogel hat einen schweren, nach unten gebogenen Schnabel und rote Augenringe. Bei Jungvögeln sind Kehle und Augenring gelblich. Der Vogel ist ein anomaler, vorwiegend auf dem Boden lebender Nashornvogel, der mit seinem Schnabel nach Reptilien, Fröschen, Insekten und kleinen Säugetieren gräbt. Sein tiefer, lauter Ruf, 'Du-Du-Dududu' ist oft frühmorgens zu hören. Aberglauben und Volkslegenden werden mit ihm verbunden.

90 cm

KRUGER

Lybius torquatus

BLACKCOLLARED BARBET (464)

This bird's bright red face and breast are surrounded by a black collar. It is a common to locally common resident. It flies on whirring wings, flicking and bobbing its wings and tail on landing. This omnivorous forager feeds predominantly on soft fruits such as papaya, figs, berries and insects. These birds make their nests in holes in trees. Both adults feed the young.

ROOIKOPHOUTKAPPER (464)

Hierdie spesie se helderrooi gesig en bors word omring deur 'n swart kraag. Hulle is algemene tot plaaslik algemene standvoëls wat in doringveld, savanne en breëblaarboswêreld voorkom. Hulle vlieg met 'n gesuis van vlerke en land met fladderende vlerke en 'n stert wat wip. Hierdie omnivoor vreet veral sagte vrugte soos papaja, vye, bessies en insekte. Hulle maak nes in gate in bome.

LE BARBU A COL NOIR (464)

Le visage et la poitrine rouge clair sont entourés d'un col noir. C'est un habitant de l'épine, de la forêt de la côte, de la savane et des pays boisés à larges feuilles dans les jardins urbains. Les oiseaux volent à toute allure, et agitent les ailes en atterrissant. Ce fouilleur omnivore se nourrit de fruits doux, de figues, de baies et d'insectes. Ces oiseaux construisent le nid dans le trou d'un arbre. Les deux adultes donnent la becquée aux jeunes à l'aide d'autres adultes.

HALSBANDBARTVOGEL (464)

Gesicht und Brust des Halsbandbartvogels sind tiefrot und von einem schwarzen Kragen umgeben. Er ist ein häufiger Bewohner der Dornsavanne, Küstenwälder, Grassteppe und breitblättriger Laubwälder und Vororte, der mit schwirrendem Flügelschlag fliegt und beim Landen mit Schwanz und Flügeln auf und nieder wippt. Dieser Allesfresser lebt vornehmlich von weichen Früchten, wie Papaya, Feigen und Beeren, und von Insekten.

Lybius torquatus

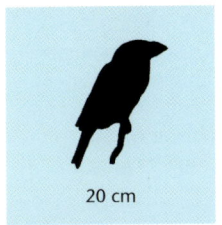

20 cm

KRUGER,
MARAKELE,
ADDO ELEPHANT

Trachyphonus vaillantii

CRESTED BARBET (473)

The yellow face, short, straggly crest and yellow underparts, streaked with red and separated by a black breast band, are diagnostic. These birds excavate their own nest holes by tearing or ripping at wood with their powerful beaks. During the breeding season they defend their nesting holes in dead branches against other species. This locally common resident feeds on insects, fruit and worms.

KUIFKOPHOUTKAPPER (473)

Die geel gesig, kort, ruie kuif en geel onderste dele wat rooi gestreep is, en geskei word deur 'n swart borsband, is diagnosties. Dit is 'n algemene standvoël wat een-een voorkom in doringveld, breëblaarboswêreld en savanne. Hulle leef van insekte, vrugte en wurms. Hierdie spesie grawe vir hom 'n gat deur die hout te skeur of stukkend te ruk met sy kragtige snawel.

LE BARBU A CRETE (473)

Le visage jaune, la crête courte et éparse, le sous-corps jaune, strié de rouge et la rayure de poitrine noire sont diagnostiques. C'est un habitant fréquent localement qui se trouve seul à l'épine, au pays boisé à larges feuilles et à la savane. Il se nourrit d'insectes, de fruits et de vers. Il excave son trou en déchirant ou en fendant le bois du bec puissant. En saison de reproduction, il défend agressivement son trou nicheur dans les branches mortes.

HAUBENBARTVOGEL (473)

Das gelbe Gesicht, die kurze, struppige Haube und die gelbe, rotgesprenkelte Unterseite mit schwarzem Brustband sind bezeichnend. Stellenweise ist er häufig; in der Dornsavanne, dem breitblättrigen Laubwald und der Grassavanne lebt er einzeln. Er ernährt sich von Insekten, Früchten und Würmern. Der Haubenbartvogel höhlt sich sein Nest in Ästen aus und verteidigt es gegen andere Vögel mit seinem starken Schnabel.

Trachyphonus vaillantii

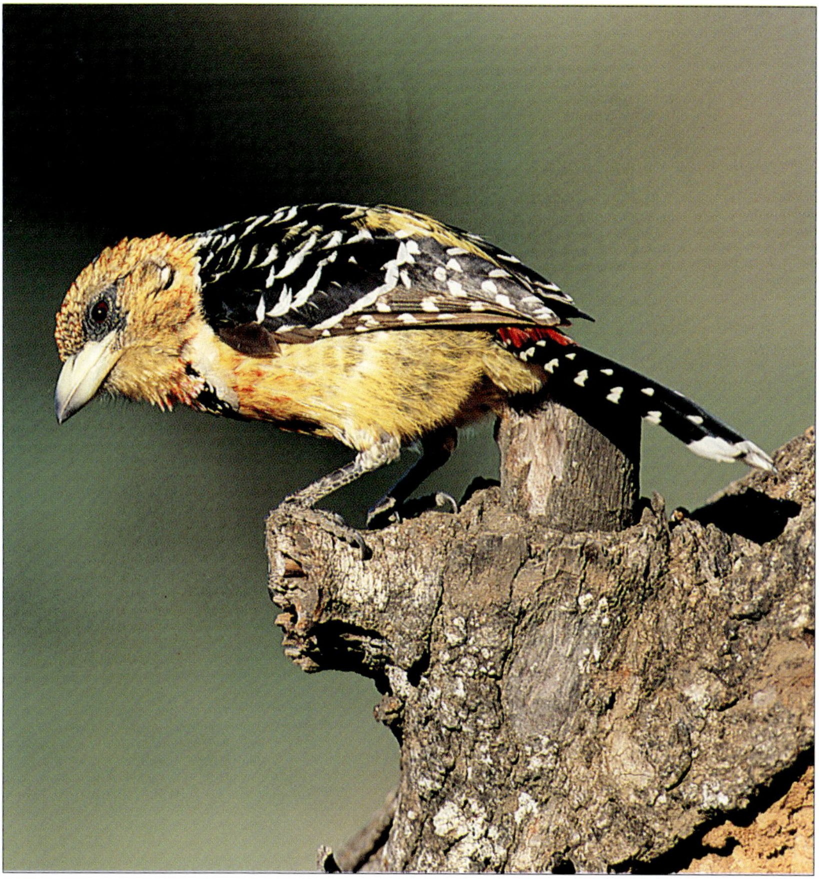

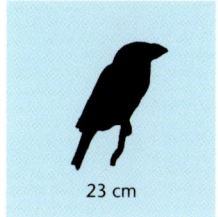

23 cm

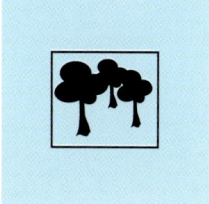

KRUGER,
\HEI-GARIEP!,
MARAKELE

Indicator indicator

GREATER HONEYGUIDE (474)

Males are unmistakable, having a pink bill and white cheek patches contrasting against a black throat and dark crown; females are a dowdy brownish grey. They will guide man to bee hives; they feed on beeswax, larval bees and other insects. They lay their eggs in the nests of other species such as kingfishers, barbets, hoopoes and bee-eaters which are left to raise the honeyguides' young.

GROOTHEUNINGWYSER (474)

Mannetjies is onmiskenbaar met hulle pienk snawel en wit wangkolle wat afsteek teen die swart keel en donker kroon. Wyfies is 'n valerige bruingrys. Hierdie voëls lei 'n mens na byekorwe – hulle leef van byewas, bylarwes en ander insekte. Hulle lê hulle eiers in ander spesies se neste, wat dan hulle kuikens moet grootmaak. Mannetjies uiter 'n singende roep, 'wiektor-wiektor'.

L'INDICATEUR (474)

Les mâles, facilement reconnaissables, ont le bec rose, les taches de joue blanches, la gorge noire et la couronne sombre; les femelles sont gris brun et ternes. Ces oiseaux conduisent l'homme à la ruche; ils se nourrissent de cire d'abeilles, d'abeilles larvaires, et d'insectes. Ils pondent leurs oeufs dans les nids d'autres espèces, comme le barbu, le guêpier et la huppe, qu'ils laissent élever leurs jeunes. Le cri, 'vic-tor, vic-tor', des mâles est sonore et perçant.

GROßER HONIGANZEIGER (474)

Die Männchen sind unverkennbar mit ihrem rosa Schnabel und den weißen Wangenflecken, die sich gegen die schwarze Kehle und den dunklen Scheitel abheben; die Weibchen haben unscheinbares braungraues Gefieder. Diese Vögel führen den Menschen zu Bienenstöcken und ernähren sich von Bienenwachs, Bienenlarven und anderen Insekten. Sie legen ihre Eier in die Nester anderer Vögel. Der ruf des Männchens ist ein schallendes 'Vik-tor, Vik-tor'.

Indicator indicator

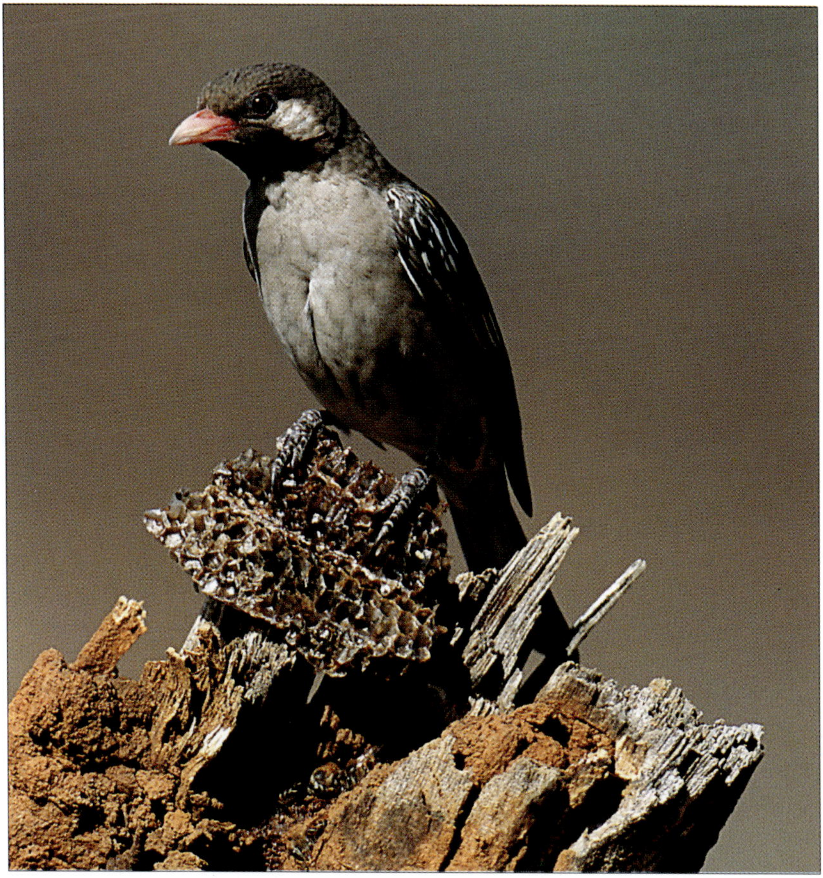

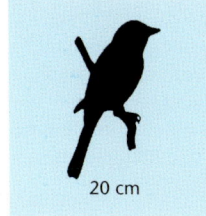

20 cm

Kruger, Marakele,
West Coast,
Karoo,
Mountain Zebra,
Bontebok,
Knysna National Lakes Area,
Wilderness, Tsitsikamma,
Golden Gate Highlands,
\Hei-!gariep

Thripias namaquus

BEARDED WOODPECKER (487)

This is the largest and only woodpecker that is barred on the breast and belly. It shows a broad, black moustache and stripe through and behind the eye; the male has a black forehead flecked with white, a red crown and a black nape while the female has an all-black forehead, crown and nape with white flecking on the forehead. Both sexes drum very loudly on resonant dead wood.

BAARDSPEG (487)

Dit is die grootste en enigste speg wat gestreep is op die bors en maag. Hierdie spesie vertoon 'n breë, swart snorstreep en 'n streep deur en agter die oog. Mannetjies het 'n swart voorkop wat wit gevlek is, 'n rooi kroon en 'n swart nek, terwyl wyfies se kroon en nek heeltemal swart is met wit vlekke op haar voorkop. Beide die geslagte trommel luid teen resonante, droë hout.

LE PIC BARBU (487)

Le plus grand pic et le seul à rayures de poitrine et de ventre, cette espèce a une large moustache noire et une rayure à travers et derrière l'oeil. Le mâle a le front noir tacheté de blanc, la couronne rouge et la nuque noire; la femelle a la nuque et la couronne noires et le front tacheté de blanc. Les deux sexes tambourinent sur le bois mort résonnant et on l'entend à un kilomètre. Ils préfèrent la savane découverte sèche et les pays boisés où ils fouillent dans des grands arbres.

NAMASPECHT (487)

Der Namaspecht ist der größte Specht und der einzige, der auf Brust und Bauch schwarzgebändert ist. Dieser Vogel hat einen breiten, schwarzen Schnurrbart und einen Augenstreifen. Das Männchen hat eine schwarze, weißgefleckte Stirn, einen roten Scheitel und einen schwarzen Nacken, während beim Weibchen die weißgefleckte Stirn, Scheitel und Nacken ganz schwarz sind. Das Klopfen dieses Spechts auf trockenes Holz ist kilometerweit zu hören.

Thripias namaquus

25 cm

KRUGER,
MARAKELE

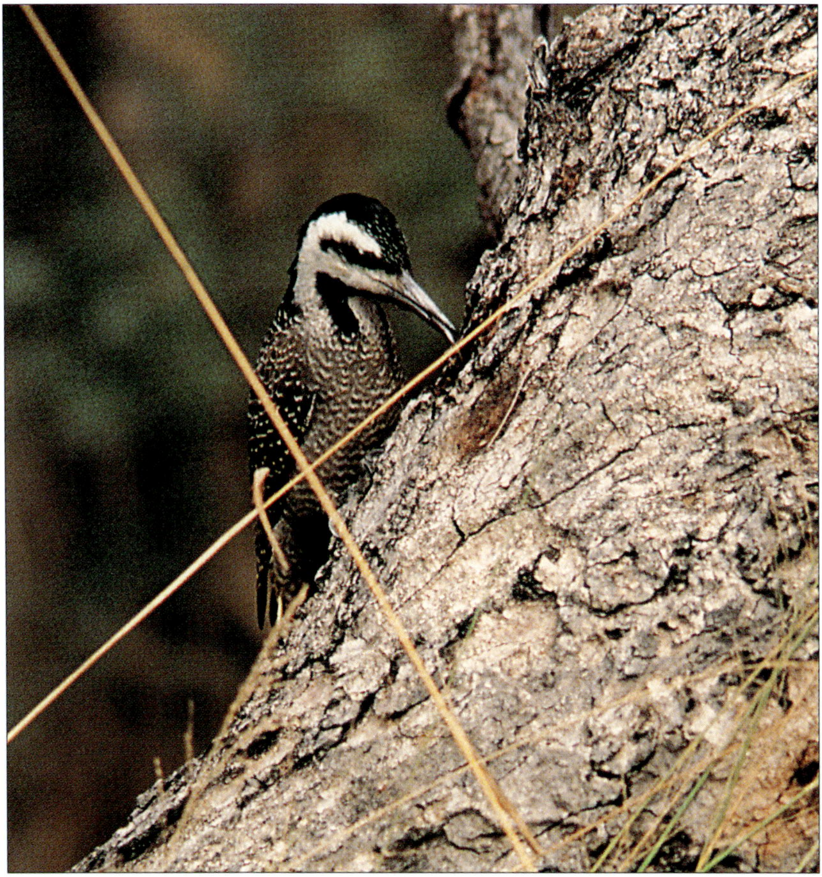

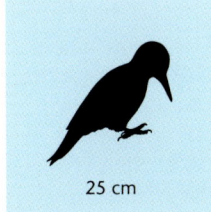

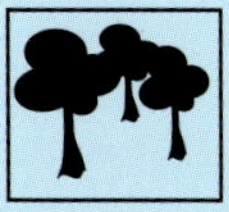

Eremopterix verticalis

GREYBACKED FINCHLARK (516)

The male has a light grey back, all-black underparts and head with a clear white cheek patch which joins a white mantle and white shoulder patch. Females are less colourful with a streaky breast, a black patch on the belly and a grey back. These common, near-endemic residents are nomadic and occur in large flocks out of the breeding season. During courtship males dangle their legs in flight.

GRYSRUGLEWERIK (516)

Mannetjies het 'n liggrys rug, heeltemal swart onderste dele en 'n kop met 'n duidelike, wit wangpatroon wat saamsmelt met 'n wit mantel en wit skouerkol. Wyfies is minder kleurvol met 'n gestreepte bors, 'n swart kol op die pens en 'n grys rug. Hierdie algemene, byna endemiese standvoëls is nomadies en kom voor in groot swerms buite die broeiseisoen.

L'ALOUETTE FRINGILLE A DOS GRIS (516)

Le mâle a le dos gris clair, le sous-corps et la tête noirs et une tache blanche attachée au manteau et à l'épaule. La femelle a la poitrine striée et une tache noire du ventre et du dos gris. Ces habitants, presque endémiques, sont nomades et se trouvent en troupeaux hors de la saison de reproduction. Ils préfèrent les prairies découvertes à l'herbe courte aux plaines de gravier. A la parade nuptiale, les pattes des mâles pendillent au vol. Ils nichent par terre.

NONNENLERCHE (516)

Das Männchen hat einen hellgrauen Rücken, eine schwarze Unterseite, einen schwarzen Kopf und einen deutlichen, weißen Wangenfleck, der in ein weißes Nackenband und weiße Schulterbänder übergeht. Weibchen sind wesentlich unscheinbarer, mit gestreifter Brust, einem schwarzen Fleck auf dem Bauch und einem grauen Rücken. Diese häufigen, nahezu endemischen Vögel sind Nomaden und treten außerhalb der Brutzeit in großen Schwärmen auf.

Eremopterix verticalis

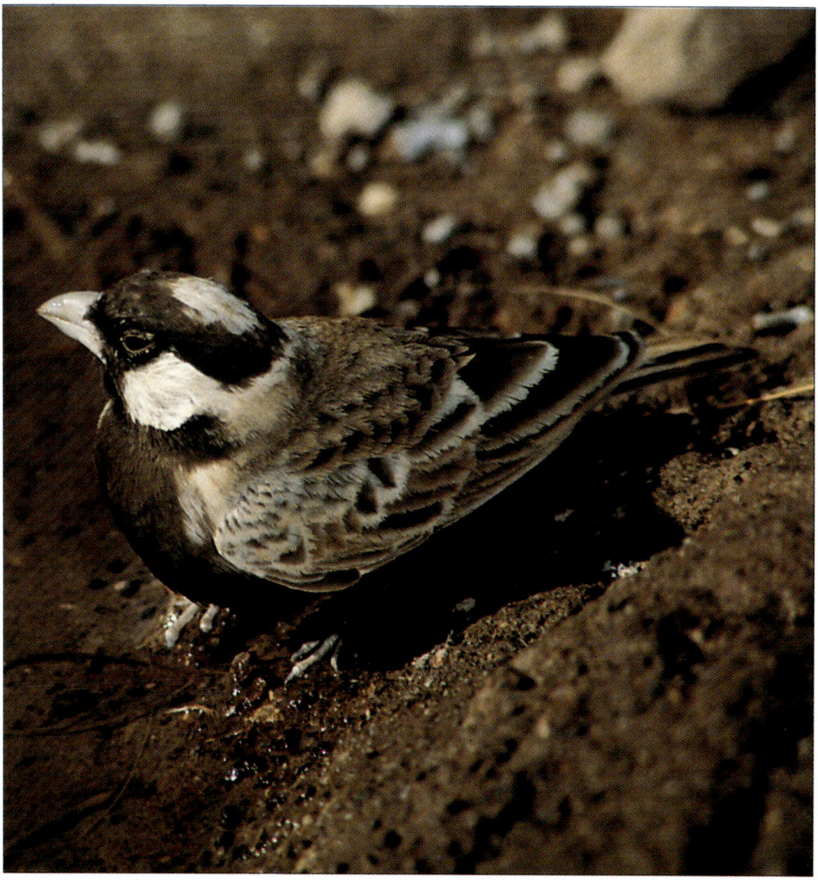

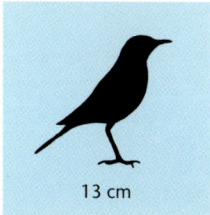

13 cm

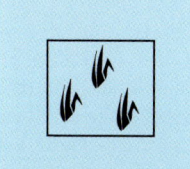

West Coast,
Tankwa Karoo,
Karoo,
Addo Elephant,
Mountain Zebra,
Kalahari Gemsbok,
Richtersveld,
Augrabies Falls

Hirundo cucullata

GREATER STRIPED SWALLOW (526)

This medium-sized swallow has a pale orange crown and rump and is lightly streaked on its pale buffy underparts. It has distinctive long tail streamers. This species is a widespread, summer visitor occurring throughout South Africa. The nest, a bowl-shaped structure made from mud pellets, and a tunnel are glued to the underside of culverts, bridges and rock overhangs on cliff faces.

GROOTSTREEPSWAEL (526)

Hierdie mediumgrootte swael is liggestreep op sy dofgeel onderste dele en het 'n bleekoranje kroon en romp. Hulle het kenmerkende, lang stertwimpels. Grootstreepswaels kom wydverspreid voor. Die nes, 'n komvormige struktuur gemaak van modderkorrels, word vasgegom aan die onderkant van geute, brûe en rotshange teen kranswande.

L'HIRONDELLE RAYEE (526)

Cette hirondelle de taille moyenne, légèrement striée au sous-corps jaune clair et pâle, a la couronne et le croupion orangé pâle, et de longues banderoles de queue distinctives. Ce visiteur répandu en été se trouve aux pays sans arbres partout en Afrique du Sud. Le nid de l'hirondelle rayée, en forme de bol, façonné de boulottes de boue, à tunnel, est collé au-dessous des canaux, des ponts et des saillies de roc aux faces des falaises.

STREIFENSCHWALBE (526)

Bei dieser mittelgroßen Schwalbe sind Scheitel und Bürzel von hellem Orange, die hellbraune Unterseite ist zart gebändert. Bezeichnend sind die langen Spieße. In ganz Südafrika sind diese Vögel weitverbreitete Sommergäste in den baumlosem Gegenden. Ihr Nest, eine schüsselartige Struktur aus Lehmklümpchen mit einem Tunnelgang, wird an unterirdische Kanäle, Brücken sowie Felsvorsprüngen an Steilwänden geklebt.

Hirundo cucullata

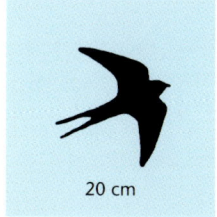

20 cm

Addo Elephant, Bontebok,
Golden Gate Highlands,
Kalahari Gemsbok, Karoo,
Knysna National Lake Area,
Kruger, Marakele, Tankwa
Karoo, Mountain Zebra,
Richtersveld, Tsitsikamma,
Augrabies Falls, \Hei-!Gariep,
West Coast, Wilderness

Dicrurus adsimilis

FORKTAILED DRONGO (541)

This distinctive bird is all black with a deeply forked tail and a red eye. It is a common resident, occurring in open woodland, thornveld, and along forest edges. An aggressive bird, it is often seen dive-bombing birds of prey in flight. This species perches on trees, catching insects in flight. It is a master at imitating the calls of other species, especially that of the Pearlspotted Owl.

MIKSTERTBYVANGER (541)

Hierdie kenmerkende voël is heeltemal swart met 'n diepgevurkte stert en 'n rooi oog. Dit is 'n algemene standvoël wat in oop boswêreld, doringveld en aan die some van woude aangetref word. Hierdie aggressiewe voël word dikwels gesien waar hy, in vlug, afpeil op roofvoëls. Hierdie spesie is 'n meesterlike nabootser van ander spesies se roepe, veral die Witkoluil s'n.

LE DRONGO A QUEUE FOURCHUE (541)

Cet oiseau distinctif tout à fait noir a la queue fortement fourchue et l'oeil rouge. Les sexes se ressemblent. C'est un habitant fréquent des pays boisés, de l'épine, des plantations exotiques, et le long des lisières des forêts. Le drongo à queue fourchue est agressif et attaque souvent en piqué les oiseaux de proie au vol. L'oiseau imite en expert les cris d'autres espèces, surtout celui de la chouette tacheté de perles.

TRAUERDRONGO (541)

Dieser auffallende Vogel ist gänzlich schwarz, hat einen tief gegabelten Schwanz und rote Augen. Er ist ein häufiger Bewohner der Dornsavanne sowie des Waldrands. Der Vogel ist aggressiv, und man kann ihn oft im Sturzflugangriff auf Greifvögel beobachten. Der Trauerdrongo ist ein Meister im Imitieren anderer Vogelrufe, insbesondere des Perlkäuzchens. Er ernährt sich von Insekten, die er im Flug oder auf dem Boden erhascht.

Dicrurus adsimilis

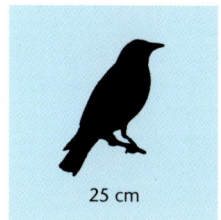

25 cm

Kruger, Marakele,
\Hei-!Gariep,
Augrabies Falls,
Kalahari Gemsbok,
Bontebok,
Knysna National Lakes Area,
Tsitsikamma, Wilderness,
Addo Elephant

Oriolus larvatus

BLACKHEADED ORIOLE (545)

A locally common resident, this species is golden yellow in colour with an all-black head and throat extending to the breast, a red bill and a red eye. Immature birds are similar except for the head and throat, which are mottled black on yellow, and the beak, which is blackish rather than coral red. These birds feed on caterpillars, most fruits and other insects, foraging in the upper canopy.

SWARTKOPWIELEWAAL (545)

Hierdie plaaslik algemene standvoël is goudgeel met 'n heeltemal swart kop en keel wat strek tot by sy bors, 'n rooi snawel en 'n rooi oog. Onvolwassenes se kop en keel is swart gespikkel, en die snawel is swarterig, nie koraalrooi nie. Hulle word aangetref in alle tipes boswêreld. Hierdie voëls vreet ruspes, vrugte en ander insekte, wat hulle in die boonste boomblaredak soek.

L'ORIOLE A TETE NOIRE (545)

Un habitant fréquent localement, l'oriole à tête noire est jaune doré à bec et à l'oeil rouges. La tête et le cou sont noirs. Les immatures ressemblent aux adultes, sauf la tête et la gorge, qui sont noires tachetées sur jaune. Ils se trouvent dans toutes sortes de pays boisés. Ces oiseaux se nourrissent de fruits et d'insectes, fouillant dans la voûte de feuillage supérieure. Un nid cupulaire, fait de lichens, d'herbe, de feuilles et d'écorce, est placé dans la fourche d'une branche.

MASKENPIROL (545)

Der Maskenpirol ist goldgelb, Kopf und Kehle sind reinschwarz bis zur Brust; er hat einen roten Schnabel und rote Augen. Die Jungvögel ähneln den Altvögeln, doch Kopf und Kehle sind gelbgestreift, der Schnabel ist eher schwärzlich. Man trifft sie in allen bewaldeten Gebieten an, aber häufiger in altem, breitblättrigem Waldland. Diese Vögel ernähren sich von Raupen, ebenso von fast allen Früchten und anderen Insekten, die sie in der Baumkronen erhaschen.

Oriolus larvatus

24 cm

BONTEBOK,
KNYSNA NATIONAL LAKES AREA,
WILDERNESS,
TSITSIKAMMA,
ADDO ELEPHANT,
KRUGER,
MARAKELE

Corvus capensis

BLACK CROW (547)

This is the only entirely black crow in the region; it has a long, slender black bill. This species feeds on grains, insects and frogs and, unlike the Pied Crow, is rarely seen scavenging in towns or at carcasses. Black Crows can be found in savanna, open grasslands, cultivated lands and drainage valleys with large trees in arid regions. The nest is a large, untidy mass of sticks sited at the top of a tree.

SWARTKRAAI (547)

Dit is die enigste heeltemal swart kraai in die streek. Die romp is slank met 'n groot, ronde kop en 'n lang, swart snawel. Hierdie spesie vreet graankorrels, insekte, paddas, en anders as by die Witborskraai, word hy selde gesien waar hy by karkasse of afvalkos in stede aas. Swartkraaie word aangetref in savanne, oop grasvelde en dreineringsvalleie. Die nes is 'n groot, slordige massa stokke.

LA CORNEILLE NOIRE (547)

La corneille noire est la seule corneille toute noire de la région. Elle a le bec noir, long et mince. Elle se nourrit de grains, d'insectes et de grenouilles, et se voit rarement fouiller en ville ou près des carcasses. La corneille noire se trouve à la savane, aux prairies découvertes, aux pays cultivés et aux vallées d'écoulement à grands arbres des régions arides. Le nid, une masse de bâtons, est au sommet d'un arbre ou d'un poteau télégraphique.

KAPKRÄHE (547)

Dies ist die einzige gänzlich schwarze Krähe der Region. Sie hat einen langen, schlanken Schnabel und ernährt sich von Körnern, Insekten und Fröschen; im Gegensatz zum Schildraben sieht man sie selten an Kadavern Aas fressen oder in den Städten. Die Nester sind große, unordentliche Strukturen aus Zweigen hoch oben in Bäumen oder auf Telegrafenmasten. Die Kapkrähe trifft man im offenen Gelände, in der Savanne, auf Feldern und in ariden Landstrichen.

Corvus capensis

50 cm

Addo Elephant, Bontebok, Golden Gate Highlands, Kalahari Gemsbok, Karoo, Knysna National Lake Area, Kruger, Marakele, Tankwa Karoo, Mountain Zebra, Richtersveld, Tsitsikamma, Augrabies Falls, \Hei-!Gariep, West Coast, Wilderness

Turdoides jardineii

ARROWMARKED BABBLER (560)

This species can be identified by its yellow to orange eye surrounded by a red ring and by the white, arrow-marked streaks on its brownish breast. Immatures lack the white streaks of the adults, and have brown eyes. This common and widespread resident can be seen in family groups of up to ten birds. It forages on the ground where it utters a cackling 'chak-chak-chak' contact call.

PYLVLEKKATLAGTER (560)

Hierdie voël kan uitgeken word aan die wit pylvlekke op sy bruinerige bors en aan die geel tot oranje oog wat omring word deur 'n rooi oogring. Onvolwasse voëls het bruin oë, maar nie die wit strepe nie. Hierdie wydverspreide standvoël word aangetref in struiksavanne en word gesien in familiegroepe van tot tien voëls. Hulle soek op die grond kos en uiter 'n 'tjak-tjak-tjak' kontakroep.

LA TIMBALIE A FLECHE (560)

Elle s'identifie par les stries blanches, marquées de flèches, à la poitrine brunâtre et à l'oeil jaune à orangé entouré d'un cercle rouge. Les immatures manquent les stries et ont les yeux bruns. Cet habitant répandu des bosquets de la savane à broussailles se voit en groupes familiales de jusqu'à dix oiseaux. Il fouille par terre et aux buissons où il pousse un cri de contact caquetant, 'chak-chak-chak'. Les nids, l'incubation des oeufs et le soin des jeunes sont des affaires de famille.

BRAUNDROSSLING (560)

Man kann diesen Vogel an seiner pfeilförmigen, weißen Zeichnung auf der bräunlichen Brust erkennen sowie an dem gelben Auge mit dem roten Augenring. Bei Jungvögeln fehlen die weißen Streifen, und sie haben braune Augen. Dieser häufiger, weitverbreitete Bewohner der Dickichte und Dornsavannen tritt in Familiengruppen auf. Sie suchen auf dem Boden und unter Büschen nach Nahrung, wo man ihren Kontaktruf, ein 'Tschak-Tschak-Tschak', hört.

Turdoides jardineii

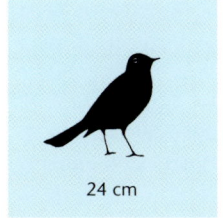

24 cm

KRUGER,
MARAKELE

Pycnonotus nigricans

REDEYED BULBUL (567)

The bright red eye wattle surrounding a dark eye is diagnostic of this species; its black cap extends to the mantle. Immatures have a pale pink eye wattle. The Redeyed Bulbul is abundant in the drier western parts of the region. This noisy species is always the first to make a fuss when it comes across a predator. It forages for fruit, nectar and insects arboreally and on the ground.

ROOIOOGTIPTOL (567)

Die helderrooi ooglel wat die donker oog omring, is diagnosties by hierdie spesie. Sy swart mus strek tot by die mantel. Onvolwassenes het 'n pienk ooglel. Dit is 'n standvoël wat volop is in die droër westelike dele van die streek. Hulle soek vrugte, nektar en insekte op die grond en in bome. Hierdie luidrugtige spesie maak altyd eerste 'n geraas as hy 'n vyand soos 'n slang teëkom.

LE BULBUL A L'OEIL ROUGE (567)

La marbrure rouge vif entourant l'oeil sombre est diagnostique; le capuchon noir s'étend au manteau. La marbrure des immatures est rose pâle. Un habitant abondant de l'ouest plus sec, cet oiseau est fréquent aux jardins, à l'épine et à la brousse près des rivières. Il fouille pour trouver des fruits, du nectar et des insectes. Cette espèce bruyante est toujours la première à faire du bruit exagéré quand elle découvre un prédateur comme un serpent ou un hibou.

MASKENBÜLBÜL (567)

Der leuchtend rote Augenring, der das dunkle Auge umgibt, kennzeichnet den Maskenbülbül; der schwarze Scheitel erstreckt sich bis zum Nacken. Jungvögel haben einen blaßrosa Augenring. Der Maskenbülbül ist in den trockeneren, westlichen Landstrichen häufig, man trifft ihn auch in Gärten, in der Dorn-savanne und in trockenem Ufergestrüpp an. Diese lärmende Vögel sind immer die ersten, die vor Schlangen oder Eulen warnen.

Pycnonotus nigricans

21 cm

RICHTERSVELD,
AUGRABIES FALLS,
KALAHARI GEMSBOK,
\HEI-!GARIEP,
KAROO,
MOUNTAIN ZEBRA

Turdus litsitsirupa

GROUNDSCRAPER THRUSH (580)

This greyish-coloured bird has boldly marked black blotches on its white underparts and a dark vertical mark through the eye. In flight it shows large, yellowish patches on the wing. On the ground this species runs quickly; it stands erect, often on a rise or a stone. It is commonly seen on lawns associated with rest camps. The call is a loud, clear and shrill whistle.

GEVLEKTE LYSTER (580)

Hierdie gryskleurige voël het duidelike swart spatsels op sy wit onderste dele en 'n donker vertikale streep deur sy oog. In vlug is groot gelerige kolle op die vlerke sigbaar. Op die grond hardloop hierdie spesie vinnig; die voël staan dikwels regop op 'n hoogte of op 'n klip. Gevlekte Lysters word dikwels gesien op grasperke by ruskampe.

LA GRIVE GRATTEUSE DE TERRE (580)

Ces oiseaux sont grisâtres. Ils ont des taches noires frappantes du sous-corps blanc et une marque sombre verticale à travers l'oeil. Cette espèce laisse voir de grandes taches jaunâtres de l'aile en volant. La grive gratteuse de terre court vite; elle reste debout, souvent sur un ressaut de terrain ou sur une pierre. Ces oiseaux se voient fréquemment aux pelouses des camps de repos. Le cri est un sifflement clair et bruyant.

AKAZIENDROSSEL (580)

Dieser gräuliche Vogel ist unten auffallend weißgesprenkelt und hat einen dunklen, senkrechten Augenstrich. Das Flugbild zeigt große, gelbliche Flecken an den Flügeln. Auf dem Boden läuft er schnell umher oder steht in besonders aufrechter Haltung, oft auf einer Anhöhe oder einem Stein. Man sieht diese Vögel viel auf den Rasenflächen in Rastlagern in arider Dornsavanne und auch in laubtragendem Waldland.

Turdus litsitsirupa

22 cm

KALAHARI GEMSBOK,
\HEI-!GARIEP,
MARAKELE,
KRUGER

Cercomela familiaris

FAMILIAR CHAT (589)

Uniformly grey in colour, the Familiar Chat habitually flicks its wings on landing, often more than once, showing its chestnut rump and outer tail feathers and the black T-shape pattern in the tail. A common and widespread chat, it is found in drier regions but occurs in all habitat types, from arid stony hills in the west to moister, hilly woodlands in the east.

GEWONE SPEKVRETER (589)

Die Gewone Spekvreter is eenvormig grys. Hierdie spesie flits sy vlerke, dikwels meer as een keer, wanneer hy land – dan is sy buitestertvere, kastaiing-bruin romp, en die swart T-patroon op sy stert sigbaar. Hulle kom algemeen en wydverspreid voor in alle habitattipes. Sy naam het ontstaan vanweë sy gewoonte om die vet te vreet wat gebruik is om ossewawiele mee te smeer.

LE TARIER (589)

Le tarier, gris uniforme, donne des chiquenades d'ailes en atterrissant, laissant voir le croupion châtain, les plumes extérieures et le 'T' noir de la queue. Un tarier fréquent répandu, on le trouve aux régions plus sèches mais on le voit dans toutes sortes d'habitat, des collines arides et rocailleuses de l'ouest aux pays boisés montagneux plus humides de l'est. Il mangeait la matière grasse utilisée pour graisser les roues des chars à boeuf, d'où le nom afrikaans.

ROSTSCHWANZSCHMÄTZER (589)

Beim Landen spreizt dieser einförmig graue Vogel mehrmals seine Flügel und zeigt das Rotbraun des Bürzels und der Außenschwanzfedern und auch das schwarze T-förmige Muster auf dem Schwanz. Man trifft diesen häufigen, weitverbreiteten Schmätzer in den trockneren Regionen an, aber er kommt fast überall vor, von den ariden, steinigen Hügeln im Westen bis zu den feuchteren, bewaldeten Hügelketten im Osten.

Cercomela familiaris

15 cm

Addo Elephant, Bontebok,
Golden Gate Highlands,
Kalahari Gemsbok, Karoo,
Knysna National Lake Area,
Kruger, Marakele, Tankwa Karoo,
Mountain Zebra, Richtersveld,
Tsitsikamma, Augrabies Falls,
\Hei-!Gariep, West Coast,
Wilderness

Cossypha caffra

CAPE ROBIN (601)

The Cape Robin shows an orange throat and vent separated by a greyish belly, and a white eyebrow. This common resident can be found on the edges of forests, in riverine bush and Karoo scrub along drainage lines. It is most often seen feeding at dusk and dawn on the edge of thick undergrowth. As the bird hops about on the ground, the tail jerks up and it flexes its wings.

GEWONE JANFREDERIK (601)

Hierdie voël toon 'n wit wenkbrou, en 'n oranje keel en kloaak wat geskei word deur 'n gryserige pens. Hierdie algemene standvoël kom aan die some van woude, in rivierbosse en Karoostruike langs dreineerpype voor. Hulle word veral tydens sonsopkoms of -ondergang gesien wanneer hulle kos soek. Terwyl die voël op die grond rondspring, wip sy stert op en sprei hy sy vlerke uit.

LE ROUGE-GORGE DU CAP (601)

Cet habitant fréquent a la gorge orangé, le ventre gris et le sourcil blanc. Il se trouve aux lisières des forêts, à la brousse des rivières, au Karoo le long des démarcations d'écoulement, au 'fynbos', aux éclaircissements des forêts et aux jardins. On le voit souvent se nourrissant à la tombée de la nuit et à l'aube aux bords du sous-bois épais. Par terre, le rouge-gorge du Cap dresse la queue et fait jouer les ailes en sautillant.

KAPRÖTEL (601)

Kehle und Kloake sind bei diesem Vogel orangegelb, er ist unten gräulich, und hat einen weißen Brauenstreifen. Meistens sieht man ihn morgens und abends in der Dämmerung, wo er am Unterholz nach Nahrung hascht.Er ist am Waldrand, im Flußufergebüsch, in Gärten, im Gestrüpp, an Bodensenken in der Karrulandschaft und in Waldlichtungen häufig. Am Boden spreizt er die Flügel, und der Schwanz schnellt nach oben.

Cossypha caffra

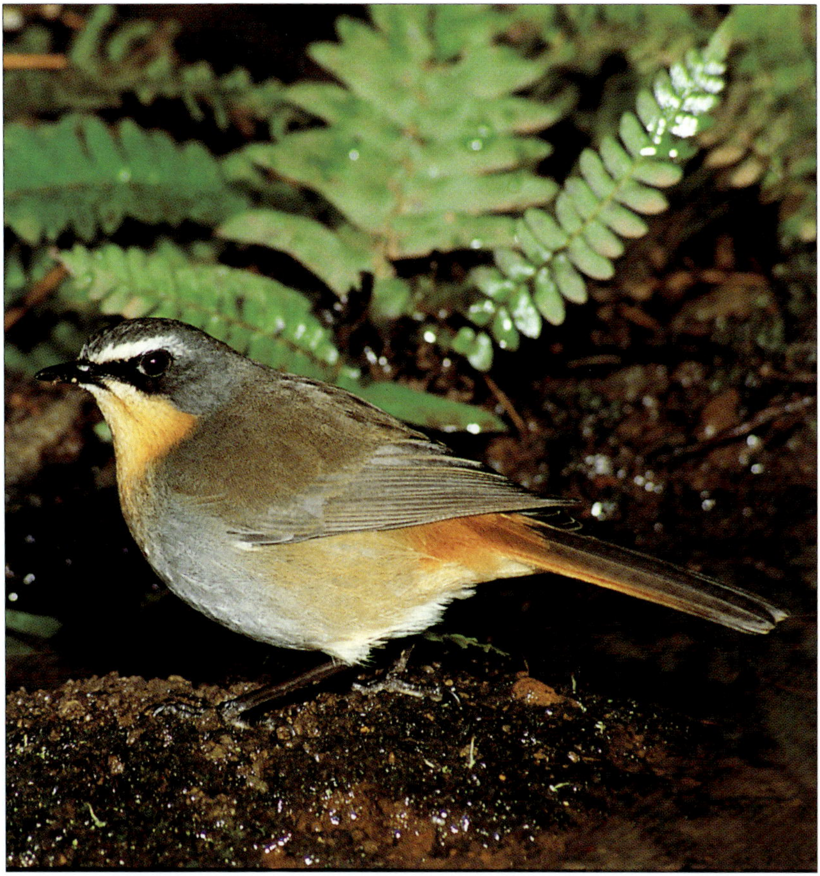

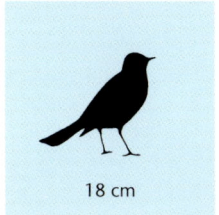

18 cm

Addo Elephant, Bontebok, Golden Gate Highlands, Kalahari Gemsbok, Karoo, Knysna National Lake Area, Kruger, Marakele, Tankwa Karoo, Mountain Zebra, Richtersveld, Tsitsikamma, Augrabies Falls, \Hei-!Gariep, West Coast, Wilderness

Terpsiphone viridis

PARADISE FLYCATCHER (710)

Male and female Paradise Flycatchers are similar. Both have a blue-black head and throat, a blue bill and eye wattle, and a chestnut back and tail. In males the tail is twice the body length, while the female's tail is as long as the body. It hawks insects from a perch in the canopy in quick, graceful forays. A breeding summer visitor, it may be found in thornveld and broadleaved woodlands.

PARADYSVLIEËVANGER (710)

Hierdie spesie het 'n blouswart kop en keel, 'n blou oogwimpel en snawel, en 'n kastaiingbruin rug en stert. By die mannetjie is die stert twee keer so lank as die liggaam, terwyl die wyfie se stert so lank soos haar lyf is. Hierdie spesie duik met grasieuse bewegings op insekte af vanwaar hulle op die rand van die blaredak sit. Die Paradysvlieëvanger is 'n somerbesoeker wat gedurende dié tyd broei.

LE GOBE-MOUCHES DE PARADIS (710)

Cet oiseau a la tête et la gorge bleu noir, le bec et la marbrure d'oeil bleus et le dos et la queue châtains – la queue du mâle a deux fois la longueur du corps; celle de la femelle est aussi longue que le corps. Cette espèce attrape des insectes d'un perchoir en raids rapides et gracieux. Un visiteur d'été qui se reproduit, il se trouve dans la brousse des rivières et de la côte, à l'épine et dans les pays boisés à larges feuilles.

PARADIESSCHNÄPPER (710)

Männliche und weibliche Paradiesschnäpper ähneln sich. Bei beiden sind Kopf und Kehle blauschwarz, sie haben einen blauen Schnabel und Augenring, Rücken und Schwanz sind kastanienfarben – beim Weibchen hat der Schwanz etwa Körperlänge, beim Männchen ist er doppelt so lang. Geschickt und graziös erjagt dieser Vogel im Flug Insekten. Als Sommergast trifft man ihn in Galerie- und Küstenwäldern, in der Dornsavanne und in breiblättrigem Waldland.

Terpsiphone viridis

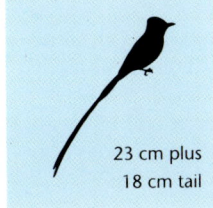

23 cm plus
18 cm tail

KRUGER,
MARAKELE,
GOLDEN GATE HIGHLANDS,
ADDO ELEPHANT,
TSITSIKAMMA,
WILDERNESS,
KNYSNA NATIONAL LAKES AREA,
BONTEBOK

131

Motacilla aguimp

AFRICAN PIED WAGTAIL (711)

This is the only black and white wagtail in the country. The upperparts are black, except for a white bar on the folded wing and a broad, white eyebrow. Immatures are duller, being grey where males are black. It forages mostly on the ground, flying or stalking about to catch moving prey. On alighting, the bird bobs its tail. It is a locally common resident and widespread throughout Africa.

BONTKWIKKIE (711)

Die Bontkwikkie is die enigste swart-en-wit kwikkie in die land. Sy bodele is swart, behalwe vir 'n wit streep op die gevoude vlerk en 'n breë, wit wenkbrou. Onvolwassenes is dowwer omdat hulle grys is op daardie dele waar mannetjies swart is. Hulle kom wydverspreid regdeur Afrika voor en is plaaslik en algemene standvoëls. Wanneer hy gaan sit of as hy gesteur word, wip hy sy stertjie.

LE BERGERONETTE DE YARRELL (711)

C'est le seul bergeronette noir et blanc du pays. Le corps supérieur est noir, sauf la bande blanche de l'aile en repos et le sourcil blanc. Les immatures sont gris, les adultes noirs. Répandu en Afrique, c'est un habitant fréquent le long des réseaux fluviaux, aux dépotoirs, aux terrains de jeu et aux jardins. Cette espèce fouille par terre, volant ou se promenant pour attraper la proie mouvante. En atterrisant, où quand il est dérangé, l'oiseau dresse et baisse la queue.

WITWENSTELZE (711)

Die Witwenstelze ist die einzige schwarzweiße Stelze im Land. Die Oberseite ist schwarz, mit Ausnahme eines weißen Streifens auf dem angelegten Flügel und einer breiten, weißen Augenbraue. Beide Geschlechter sehen gleich aus. Jungvögel sind unscheinbarer. Sie sind in ganz Afrika verbreitet und leben an Flußläufen und Kläranlagen, auf Schulhöfen und in Gärten. Wenn er aufgestört wird und sich in die Luft schwingt, wippt der Vogel mit dem Schwanz.

Motacilla aguimp

20 cm

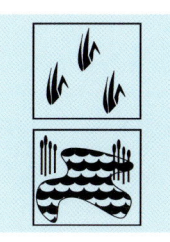

Kruger,
Marakele,
\Hei-!gariep,
Augrabies Falls,
Richtersveld,
Addo Elephant,
Golden Gate Highlands

Lanius collaris

FISCAL SHRIKE (732)

This black and white shrike has a longish tail. Males are all white below, while females have a small chestnut patch on the lower flank. Individuals found in the arid west show a prominent white eyebrow. It is a widespread resident of grasslands and woodlands. An opportunist, it feeds on insects, frogs, lizards and small snakes. It often impales its prey on thorns and returns to feed on it later.

FISKAALLAKSMAN (732)

Hierdie swart-en-wit laksman het 'n langerige stert. Mannetjies is heeltemal wit aan die onderkant, terwyl wyfies 'n klein, kastaiingbruin kol op die laer flank het. Individuele voëls in die droë weste het 'n prominente wit wenkbrou. Hierdie standvoël kom wydverspreid voor op grasvelde en in boswêreld. Hy vreet slangetjies, insekte, paddas en akkedisse wat hy deurboor met 'n doring.

LA PIE-GRIECHE FISCALE (732)

Cette pie noire est blanche à la queue assez longue. Le mâle est blanc dessous, la femelle a une petite tache châtaine au flanc inférieur. Les oiseaux de l'ouest aride ont le sourcil blanc. C'est un habitant répandu des prairies boisés, des buissons épars, de l'épine et des jardins. Opportuniste, il se nourrit d'insectes et de petits reptiles. Il impale souvent sa proie sur une épine, le fil de fer barbelé ou une brindille aiguë. On l'appelle 'Jeannot Bourreau' ou 'l'oiseau boucher'.

FISKALWÜRGER (732)

Dieser schwarzweiße Würger hat einen länglichen Schwanz. Das Männchen ist unten reinweiß, während das Weibchen einen kleinen rotbraunen Fleck an der Unterflanke hat. In arideren Gebieten haben diese Vögel eine auffälligen, weißen Brauenstreifen. Die Art ist weitverbreitet in der Baumsavanne, der Dornsavanne, in Gärten und in Halbwüsten. Der Fiskalwürger lebt von Insekten, Fröschen, Eidechsen und kleinen Schlangen. Oft spießt er seine Beute auf.

Lanius collaris

23 cm

Addo Elephant, Bontebok, Golden Gate Highlands, Kalahari Gemsbok, Karoo, Knysna National Lake Area, Kruger, Marakele, Tankwa Karoo, Mountain Zebra, Richtersveld, Tsitsikamma, Augrabies Falls, \Hei-!Gariep, West Coast, Wilderness

Laniarius atrococcineus

CRIMSONBREASTED SHRIKE (739)

The crimson underparts of this bird contrast sharply with the nearly all-black upperparts; the white bar through the wing is distinctive. The Crimsonbreasted Shrike occurs in thornveld and semi-arid scrub in the central and arid western parts of the country. It forages for insects on the ground and in trees. Its clear, liquid whistle is a characteristic call of the bushveld.

ROOIBORSLAKSMAN (739)

Die karmosynrooi onderste dele van hierdie voël steek skerp af teen die amper heeltemal swart bodele. Die wit streep deur die vlerk is kenmerkend. Hulle kom voor in doringveld en semidroë struikgewas in die sentrale en droë, westelike dele van die land. Hierdie voëls soek insekte op die grond en in bome. Sy helder, vloeiende fluit is 'n kenmerkende roep in die bosveld.

LA PIE-GRIECHE A GORGE ROUGE (739)

Le corps supérieur de la pie-grièche à gorge rouge est cramoisi et le corps inférieur presque tout noir; la bande blanche à travers l'aile est distinctive. Cet oiseau se trouve dans l'épine et dans la brousse semi-aride des régions centrales et arides de l'ouest. Il fouille par terre et dans les arbres pour trouver des insectes. Le sifflement clair et harmonieux de cette espèce est un son typique de la brousse.

ROTBAUCHWÜRGER (REICHSVOGEL) (739)

Die karminrote Unterseite des Vogels hebt sich von der nahezu gänzlich schwarzen Oberseite ab; auffällig ist das weiße Flügelfeld. Der Rotbauchwürger kommt in der Dornsavanne und in der Halbwüste im ariden Westen vor. Auf dem Boden und in den Bäumen macht er Jagd auf Insekten. Wegen seines schwarzweißroten Gefieders heißt er im Volksmund Reichsvogel. Sein klarer Flötenton ist ein charakteristischer Ruf im Busch.

Laniarius atrococcineus

23 cm

Marakele,
Kalahari Gemsbok,
Augrabies Falls,
Richtersveld,
\Hei-!gariep

Prionops plumatus

WHITE HELMETSHRIKE (753)

The unmistakable White Helmetshrike has pure white underparts, a bright yellow eye ring surrounding a yellow iris, and a grey mantle and crown. This gregarious species utters a series of loud clicks as it flies quickly from bush to bush in an undulating manner. In flight the white lines in the wings and white outer tail feathers contrast against the otherwise black wings and back.

WITHELMLAKSMAN (753)

Hierdie onmiskenbare spesie het spierwit onderste dele, 'n heldergeel oogring wat die geel iris omring, en 'n grys mantel en kroon. Hulle kom gewoonlik voor in groepe van ses tot 15. Hierdie voëls uiter 'n reeks harde klikke wanneer hulle vinnig van bos tot bos vlieg met 'n golwende beweging. In vlug kontrasteer die wit lyne op die vlerke en die wit buitestertvere met die swart rug en vlerke.

LE BAGADAIS BLANC (753)

Facile à reconnaître, le bagadais blanc a le sous-corps tout blanc, un cercle d'oeil jaune autour de l'iris jaune et le manteau et la couronne gris. Vus d'habitude en troupeaux de six à 15, ces oiseaux poussent une série de clics à haute voix en volant rapidement d'un buisson à l'autre d'une manière ondulante. Au vol, les lignes blanches des ailes et des plumes blanches de la queue extérieure contrastent avec le noir.

BRILLENWÜRGER (753)

Der unverwechselbare Brillenwürger hat eine reinweiße Unterseite; ein leuchtend gelber Hautring umrandet eine gelbe Iris, Scheitel und Halsband sind grau. Die Vögel kommen gewöhnlich in Scharen von sechs bis fünfzehn Stück vor; sie stoßen laute, zirpende Rufe aus, während sie eilig, wellenförmig von Strauch zu Strauch schwirren. Im Flug heben sich die weißen Flügelstreifen und die Außenschwanzfedern von dem sonst schwarzen Rückengefieder ab.

20 cm

KRUGER,
MARAKELE

Creatophora cinerea

WATTLED STARLING (760)

This nomadic, greyish-brown starling with its pale rump is usually seen in large flocks. Adult males have a black crown and facial wattles with an extensive yellow hindcrown. Females and non-breeding males are duller and do not have the wattles, but show a small yellow patch below and behind the eye. In flight these birds appear grey with a white rump and black flight feathers.

LELSPREEU (760)

Hierdie nomadiese, grysbruin spreeu met sy ligte romp word gewoonlik in groot swerms aangetref. Volwasse mannetjies het 'n swart kroon en swart gesiglelle met 'n uitgestrekte, geel agterkroon. Wyfies en nie-broeiende mannetjies is vaal en het nie lelle nie, maar vertoon 'n klein, geel kol onder en agter die oog. In vlug lyk hulle grys met 'n wit romp en swart vlerke.

L'ETOURNEAU CARONCULE (760)

Cet étourneau gris brun nomade a le croupion pâle. Les mâles adultes ont la couronne noire, le visage marbré et l'arrière-couronne jaune et étendue. Les femelles et les mâles non-reproducteurs sont moins colorés, sans marbrure. Ils ont une petite tache jaune derrière et au-dessous de l'oeil. Au vol, ils sont gris au croupion blanc et aux plumes de vol noires. Ils se juchent et se nichent ensemble dans les arbres et ils volent ensemble en troupeaux serrés.

LAPPENSTAR (760)

Diesen nomadischen, graubraunen Star mit hellem Bürzel sieht man gewöhnlich in großen Schwärmen. In der Brutzeit haben Männchen einen schwarzen Scheitel und Kehllappen und einen gelben Hinterkopf. Das Schlichtkleid ist bei beiden Geschlechtern unscheinbarer, auch fehlt der Kehllappen. Gelbe Flecken sind unter und hinter den Augen sichtbar. Das Flugbild wirkt grau, der Bürzel ist weiß, die Schwungfedern sind schwarz.

Creatophora cinerea

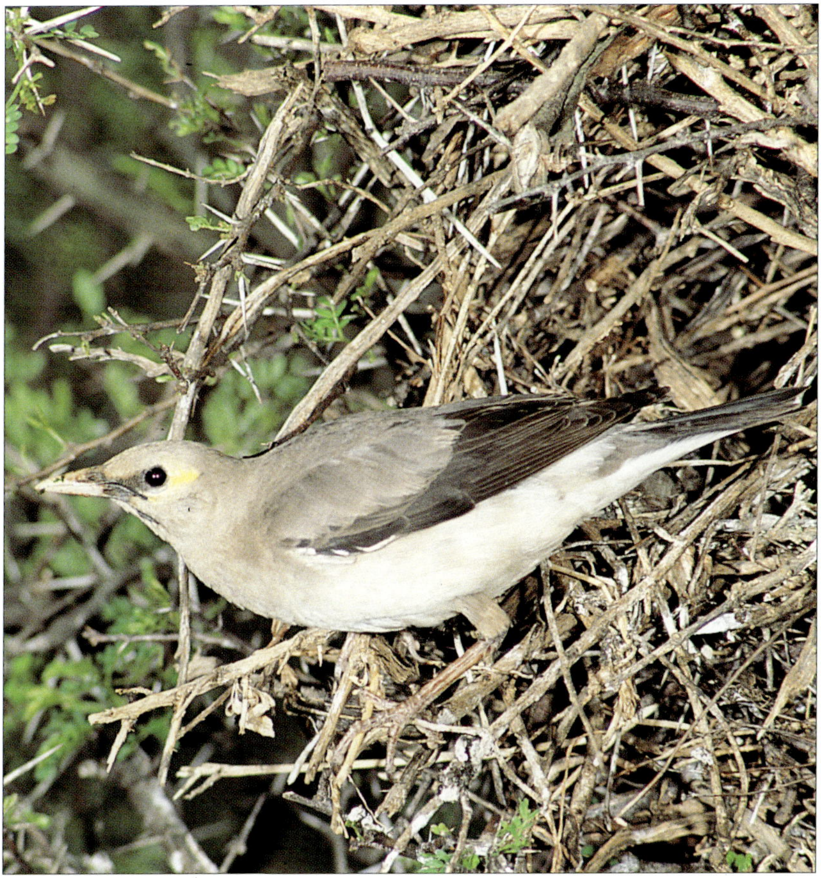

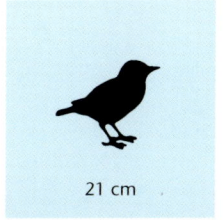

21 cm

Addo Elephant,
Golden Gate Highlands,
Kalahari Gemsbok, Karoo,
Kruger, Marakele, Tankwa Karoo,
Mountain Zebra, Richtersveld,
Augrabies Falls, \Hei-!gariep,
West Coast

Lamprotornis nitens

GLOSSY STARLING (764)

As an adult, the Glossy Starling has a yellow-orange eye. It has an overall glossy green colour, including the ear coverts and belly. The sexes are alike. Immatures are similar to adults, but are blacker, less iridescent and have a brownish eye. This species is the commonest and most widespread blue starling in the country. It feeds on insects, fruits and plant nectars, from aloes for example.

KLEINGLANSSPREEU (764)

Volwasse Kleinglansspreeus het 'n geeloranje oog. Hy is oraloor glansgroen, insluitende die oordekvere en pens. Die geslagte lyk eners. Onvolwassenes lyk soos volwassenes, maar is swarter, minder reënboogkleurig en het 'n bruinerige oog. Hierdie spesie is die algemeenste en wydverspreidste blouspreeu in die land. Hulle vreet insekte, vrugte en plantnektar, soos aalwynnektar.

LE LAMPROCOLIOU (764)

L'adulte a l'oeil jaune orangé. En général, il est vert brillant, y compris les couverts d'oreille et le ventre. Les deux sexes se ressemblent. Les immatures ressemblent aux adultes, mais ils sont plus noirs, moins iridescents, et ont l'oeil brunâtre. C'est l'espèce d'étourneau bleu le plus fréquent et répandu du pays. Il se nourrit de fruits, d'insectes et de nectar des plantes comme des aloès. Le cri est 'trrr-chree-chrrrr'.

ROTSCHULTERGLANZSTAR (764)

Ausgewachsen hat der Rotschulterglanzstar orangegelbe Augen. Er hat ein durchgehend grünschillerndes Federkleid, einschließlich der Ohrendeckfedern und des Bauches. Die Geschlechter sehen gleich aus. Jungvögel ähneln den Altvögeln aber sie sind schwärzer, weniger schillernd und haben bräunliche Augen. Dies ist der häufigste und am weitesten verbreitete Glanzstar im Land. Er lebt gesellig in Dornsavanne, Mischwald und am Stadtrand.

Lamprotornis nitens

25 cm

Richtersveld, Augrabies Falls, Kalahari Gemsbok, \Hei-!gariep, Tankwa Karoo, Karoo, Mountain Zebra, Addo Elephant, Marakele, Golden Gate Highlands, Wilderness, Bontebok, Knysna National Lakes Area, Tsitsikamma, Kruger

Buphagus erythrorhynchus

REDBILLED OXPECKER (772)

This species has an all-red bill and a bright yellow eye wattle which surrounds a red eye; in flight it shows a uniform dark rump. Young birds are the same colour but have a brown bill and a dark brown eye. It is likely to be seen on antelope species, giraffe and cattle where it feeds on dried blood around wounds, flies and ticks. This bird feeds by combing the hair of the host with its sharp bill.

ROOIBEKRENOSTERVOËL (772)

Hierdie spesie het 'n rooi snawel en 'n heldergeel ooglel, wat die rooi oog omring. In vlug is 'n eenvormige, donker romp sigbaar. Jong voëls het dieselfde kleur, maar het 'n bruin snawel en 'n donkerbruin oog. Dit is 'n algemene standvoël in wildreservate. Hulle word gewoonlik aangetref op wildsbokspesies, kameelperde en vee waar hulle bosluise, vlieë en droë bloed om wonde vreet.

LE PIQUE-BOEUF A BEC ROUGE (772)

Le bec est tout rouge, la marbrure entourant l'oeil rouge est jaune. Au vol, il laisse voir le croupion sombre uniforme. Les jeunes ont le bec brun et l'oeil brun sombre. C'est un habitant fréquent des réserves naturelles, pas des régions d'élevage où les insecticides toxiques et les bains parasiticides ont réduit leur nombre. Cet oiseau peut se voir sur les antilopes, sur les giraffes et sur le bétail où il se nourrit de tiques, de mouches et de sang séché autour des blessures.

ROTSCHNABELMADENHACKER (772)

Diese Vögel haben rote Schnäbel und leuchtend gelbe Hautringe um die roten Augen. Das Flugbild zeigt den einheitlich dunklen Bürzel. Jungvögel sehen ähnlich aus, aber sie haben braune Schnäbel und dunkelbraune Augen. Diese Art ist in den Wildschutzgebieten häufig, aber dort wo Rinderzucht betrieben wird, reduzierten Pestizide ihre Anzahl drastisch. Man kann ihn auf Wildtieren und Rindern sehen, wo er von Zecken, Fliegen und verkrustetem Wundblut lebt.

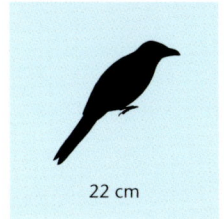

22 cm

Kruger,
Marakele

Plocepasser mahali

WHITEBROWED SPARROW-WEAVER (799)

This bird can be identified by its broad, white eyebrow, diagnostic white rump (seen in flight) and its loud, liquid 'cheeop-preeooo-chop' call notes. It is a common resident, occurring in dry thornveld and bare regions. The untidy, straw-like nest is indicative of its presence in an area. Usually seen in pairs or small groups, these birds forage on the ground and roost at night in their nests.

KORINGVOËL (799)

Koringvoëls word uitgeken aan hulle breë, wit wenkbrou, diagnostiese wit romp en luide, vloeiende 'tjeeoop-preeoo-tjop'-roep. Dit is 'n algemene standvoël wat in droë doringveld en oorbeweide streke voorkom. Die slordige, strooiagtige nes is kenmerkend van sy teenwoordigheid. Hulle word in pare of klein groepe gesien; hulle soek kos op die grond en slaap snags in die nes.

LE TISSERIN MOINEAU A SOURCILS BLANCS (799)

On identifie cet oiseau au large sourcil blanc, au croupion blanc diagnostique (vu au vol) et aux notes résonnantes et harmonieuses de son cri, 'cheeoppreeooo-chop'. Le tisserin moineau à sourcils blancs est un habitant fréquent de l'épine sèche des régions dénudées, dépouillées et surpâtrées. Le nid débraillé ressemble à la paille et indique sa présence. On les voit en petits groupes, fouillant par terre. Ils se juchent la nuit dans leur nid.

MAHALIWEBER (799)

Den Mahaliweber erkennt man an seinen breiten, weißen Brauenstreifen, dem bezeichnenden weißen Bürzel (sichtbar im Flug) und seinem lauten, wohltönenden Ruf, 'Tschieuup-Prieeu-Tschop'. Er ist ein häufiger Bewohner der Dornsavanne und kahler, abgeweideter Gebiete. Das unordentliche, strohige Nest verrät seine Anwesenheit. Die Vögel treten gewöhnlich paarweise oder in Grüppchen auf. Sie suchen auf dem Boden nach Nahrung.

Plocepasser mahali

19 cm

MARAKELE,
\HEI-!GARIEP,
MOUNTAIN ZEBRA,
AUGRABIES FALLS,
KALAHARI GEMSBOK

Passer melanurus

CAPE SPARROW (803)

Males are unmistakable with their black and white heads; females are duller, lacking the distinctive black head but retaining the chestnut back, which distinguishes them from other sparrow species. It is a common resident in Karoo scrub, grasslands and along watercourses. They forage for grains and insects by hopping on the ground, frequently in the company of weavers.

GEWONE MOSSIE (803)

Gewone Mossies met hulle swart-en-wit koppe is onmiskenbaar. Wyfies is valer, en het nie die kenmerkende swart kop nie, maar hulle het wel 'n kastaiingbruin rug wat hulle onderskei van ander mossiespesies. Hierdie voël is 'n algemene standvoël in Karoostruikgewasse en kom ook voor op grasvelde, doringveld en waterweë. Hulle soek graankorrels en insekte deur op die grond rond te spring.

LE MOINEAU DU CAP (803)

Le mâle est facilement reconnaissable à la tête noire et blanche. La femelle moins colorée manque la tête noire distinctive mais a le dos châtain qui le séparent d'autres espèces de moineau. Cet oiseau habite généralement la brousse du Karoo, les prairies, l'épine, les jardins et le long des cours d'eau et n'est jamais loin de l'eau. Il fouille pour trouver des grains et des insectes en sautant par terre, fréquemment avec des moineaux et des tisserins.

KAPSPERLING (803)

Der männliche Kapsperling ist mit seinem schwarzweiß gezeichneten Kopf unverkennbar; die Weibchen sind unscheinbarer, ohne den auffälligen, schwarzen Kopf, weisen aber auch das kastanienbraune Rückengefieder auf, was sie von anderen Sperlingen unterscheidet. Diese Vögel sind häufig in der Karru, im Grasland, in der Dornsavanne, in Gärten und an Flußläufen; sie sind nie weit vom Wasser entfernt.

Passer melanurus

15 cm

RICHTERSVELD, AUGRABIES FALLS,
KALAHARI GEMSBOK, \HEI-!GARIEP,
TANKWA KAROO, KAROO, MOUNTAIN ZEBRA,
WEST COAST, BONTEBOK,
KNYSNA NATIONAL LAKES AREA,
WILDERNESS, ADDO ELEPHANT,
GOLDEN GATE HIGHLANDS,
TSITSIKAMMA, MARAKELE

Ploceus velatus

SOUTHERN MASKED WEAVER (814)

Males have a black face with a red eye and a uniform greenish back. Females are generally dull brown, with a greenish back and a brown eye. In summer males have a distinctive summer suit, but in winter they lose this plumage and look like the female. They build a distinctive nest – a coarsely woven ball without an entrance tunnel, often overhanging water. The call is a harsh, swizzling sound.

SWARTKEELGEELVINK (814)

Mannetjies het 'n swart gesig met 'n rooi oog en 'n eenvormig, groenerige rug. Wyfies is oor die algemeen vaalbruin met 'n groenerige rug en 'n bruin oog. In die somer het mannetjies 'n kenmerkende somerkleed, maar in die winter verloor hulle hierdie verekleed en lyk hulle nes die wyfies. Hierdie spesie kom wydverspreid voor. Die nes is 'n grofgeweefde bal sonder 'n ingangstonnel.

LE TISSERIN MASQUE (814)

Les mâles ont le visage noir, l'oeil rouge et le dos verdâtre uniforme. Les femelles sont généralement brunes et ternes, au dos verdâtre et à l'oeil brun. En été les mâles ont leur plumage d'été distinctif, mais ils le perdent en hiver quand ils ressemblent à la femelle. Cet oiseau est répandu partout dans la région. Le nid distinctif – une pelote rudement lissée sans tunnel d'entrée – est souvent suspendu au-dessus de l'eau. Le cri rauque et grésillant est 'chik-chik'.

MASKENWEBER (814)

Männchen haben ein schwarzes Gesicht mit roten Augen und einen olivgrünen Rücken. Weibchen sind meist unscheinbar braun, mit grünlichem Rücken und braunen Augen. Die Männchen tragen ein Sommerkleid, aber im Winter sehen sie aus wie die Weibchen. Diese Art ist in der ganzen Region weitverbreitet. Die Vögel bauen ein auffallendes Nest – eine grobgewebte Kugel ohne Eingangs-tunnel, die oft über dem Wasser schwebt. Der Ruf ist ein hartes Zwitschern.

Ploceus velatus

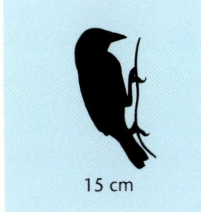

15 cm

Addo Elephant, Bontebok, Golden Gate Highlands, Kalahari Gemsbok, Karoo, Knysna National Lake Area, Kruger, Marakele, Tankwa Karoo, Mountain Zebra, Richtersveld, Tsitsikamma, Augrabies Falls, \Hei-!Gariep, West Coast, Wilderness

Euplectes orix

RED BISHOP (824)

Males in breeding plumage have a distinctive bright red head and back, a black face and black belly. Non-breeding males resemble females and immatures which are dull brown with dark brown streaks on the back, distinct dark streaks on the pale brown breast and belly, and a pale, whitish eyebrow. Red Bishops feed on the ground, walking in short steps to search for seeds and insects.

ROOIVINK (824)

Broeiende mannetjies het 'n kenmerkende helderrooi kleur, 'n swart gesig en swart pens. Die vere van nie-broeiende mannetjies lyk nes dié van wyfies en onvolwassenes. Hulle het donkerbruin strepe op die rug, duidelike swart strepe op die bleekbruin bors en pens, en 'n bleek, witterige wenkbrou. Hulle gee kort treetjies terwyl hulle op die grond na saadjies en insekte soek.

L'ONYX GRENADIER (824)

Les mâles en plumage de reproduction sont rouges, et noirs au visage et au ventre. Les autres ressemblent aux femelles à rayures sombres du dos, de la poitrine et du ventre et à sourcil pâle et blanchâtre. Ils se réunissent en grands troupeaux quand ils ne se reproduisent pas. Les mâles se voient le plus souvent aux roselières, les ailes battant rapidement, en poussant un cri bourdonnant et gai. Ils se trouvent à l'herbe longue, trop drue et aux pays cultivés.

ORYXWEBER (824)

Im Brutkleid haben Männchen ein auffälliges, rotes Gefieder, Gesicht und Bauch sind schwarz. Im Schlichtkleid ähneln die Männchen den Weibchen und Jung-vögeln. Sie haben dunkelbraune Streifen auf dem Rücken, auf der hellbraunen Brust und auf dem Bauch, und weisen einen hellen, weißlichen Brauenstreifen auf. Bei der Nahrungssuche trippeln sie auf dem Boden umher und suchen nach Samen und Insekten. Dieser gefräßige Vogel tritt in großen Schwärmen auf.

Euplectes orix

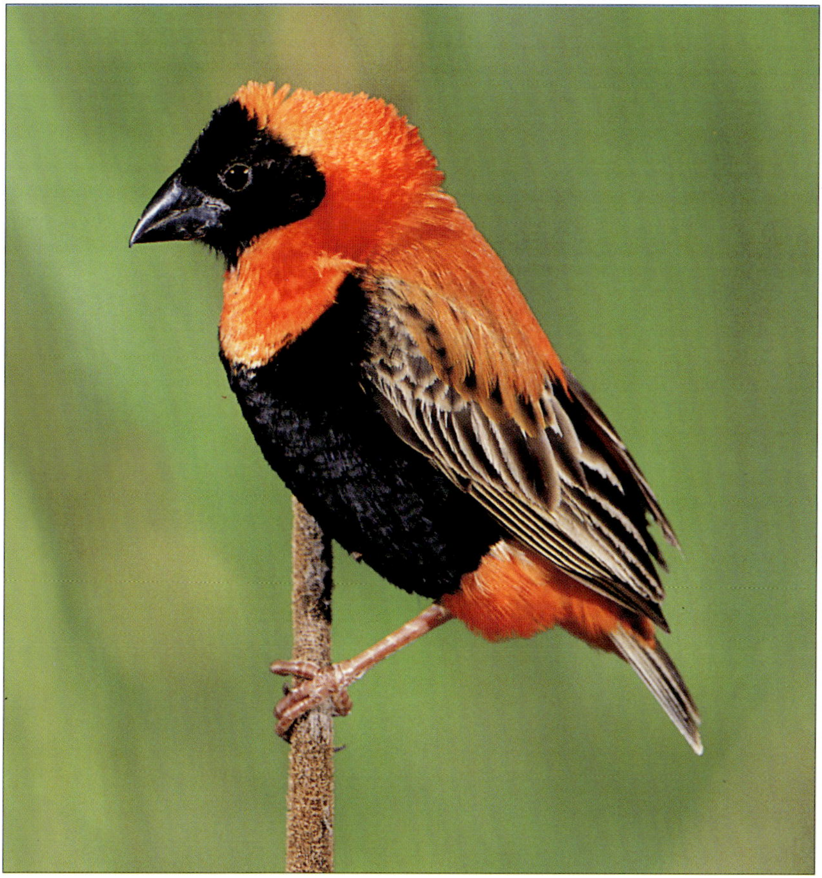

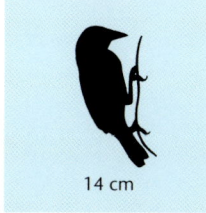

14 cm

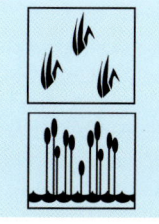

Richtersveld, Augrabies Falls,
West Coast, \Hei-!Gariep,
Bontebok, Karoo,
Wilderness, Addo Elephant,
Mountain Zebra,
Golden Gate Highlands,
Knysna National Lakes Area,
Kruger

Euplectes progne

LONGTAILED WIDOW (832)

Females, non-breeding males and immatures are mottled buffy brown, streaked with black. Breeding males are all black with an exceptionally long, broad tail. These birds occur in grassland regions, especially damp locations. The laboured flight action shows broad, rounded wings, a long floppy tail and a red shoulder patch. When breeding, the males have approximately five females each.

LANGSTERTFLAP (832)

Wyfies, nie-broeiende mannetjies en onvolwassenes is bont, liggeelbruin met swart strepe. Broeiende mannetjies is heeltemal swart met 'n buitengewone lang, breë stert. Hierdie voëls kom in grasveldstreke, veral vogtige plekke voor. Tydens hulle moeisame vliegaksie uiter hulle 'n 'zzit-zzit'-geluid en toon breë, geronde vlerke, 'n lang, slap stert en 'n rooi skouerkol.

LA VEUVE GEANTE (832)

Les femelles, les mâles reproducteurs et les immatures sont bruns, marbrés, et striés de noir. Les mâles reproducteurs sont noirs à la queue large et très longue. Chaque mâle a environ cinq femelles. Ces oiseaux se trouvent dans les prairies, surtout humides. Le vol laborieux révèle les ailes larges et arrondies, la longue queue pendante et la tache d'épaule rouge. Les mâles se juchent ensemble la nuit, poussant un 'zik-zik-zik-zik' au vol.

HAHNENSCHWEIFWIDA (832)

Im Brutkleid sind die Männchen reinschwarz und haben einen außergewöhnlich langen, breiten Schwanz. Die Weibchen, Jungvögel und Männchen im Schlichtkleid sind beigebraungesprenkelt mit dunklen Streifen. Dieser Vogel lebt in Grasfluren, besonders in feuchten Gebieten. Bei der unbeholfenen Flugbewegung gewahrt man die breiten, abgerundeten Flügel sowie den biegsamen Schwanz und einen roten Schulterfleck.

Euplectes progne

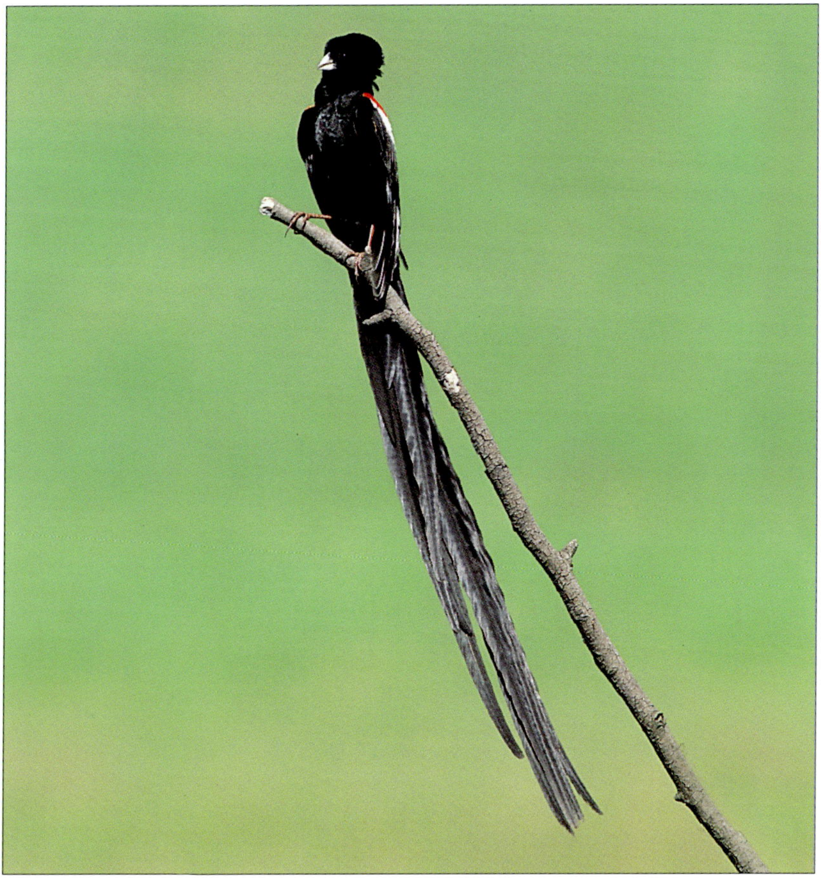

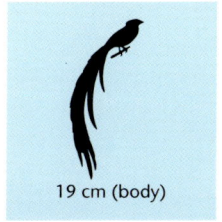

19 cm (body)

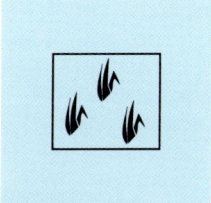

MARAKELE,
GOLDEN GATE HIGHLANDS,
ADDO ELEPHANT,
MOUNTAIN ZEBRA

Vidua macroura

PINTAILED WHYDAH (860)

Breeding males are unmistakable, being black above and pure white below, and having a bright pink bill and four long, black tail feathers. Non-breeding males and females are buffy brown with black streaking, two black crown stripes, a greyish-pink bill and black legs. Males are polygamous, having up to five females. This species is widespread throughout the country.

KONINGROOIBEKKIE (860)

Broeiende mannetjies is onmiskenbaar vanweë hulle swart bodele en spierwit onderste dele, 'n helderpienk snawel en vier lang, swart stertvere. Wyfies en nie-broeiende mannetjies is liggeelbruin met swart strepe, twee swart kroonstrepe, 'n gryspienk snawel en swart bene. Mannetjies is poligaam, en het tot vyf wyfies gedurende die broeiseisoen. Hulle is wydverspreid dwarsdeur die land.

LA VEUVE DOMINICAINE (860)

Les mâles reproducteurs noirs et blancs, faciles à reconnaître, ont le bec rose et quatre plumes de queue longues et noires. Les femelles et les mâles non-reproducteurs sont brun roux à stries noires, à deux raies noires de la couronne, à bec rose gris et à pattes noires. Les mâles sont polygames et ont jusqu'à cinq femelles en saison reproductrice. Répandue à travers le pays, cette espèce vit en parasite à la savane et aux prairies sur les astrilds, les spermètes et les cisticolas.

DOMINIKANERWITWE (860)

Im Brutkleid sind die Männchen unverkennbar: oben schwarz und unten rein-weiß, der Schnabel ist leuchtend rosa und die vier langen Schwanzfedern sind schwarz. Im Schlichtkleid sehen die Männchen wie die Weibchen aus, gelb-braun und schwarzgestreift, auf dem Scheitel sind zwei schwarze Streifen. Der Schnabel ist rosagrau und die Beine sind schwarz. Die Männchen sind polygam und haben in der Brutzeit bis zu fünf Weibchen.

Vidua macroura

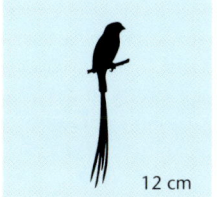

12 cm

Augrabies Falls, West Coast,
Tankwa Karoo, Karoo,
\Hei-!Gariep, Mountain Zebra,
Knysna National Lakes Area,
Tsitsikamma, Wilderness,
Addo Elephant, Kruger,
Golden Gate Highlands,
Marakele, Bontebok

Emberiza flaviventris

GOLDENBREASTED BUNTING (884)

The Goldenbreasted Bunting can be identified by its black and white striped head, chestnut mantle and golden-yellow breast which is brighter in males than in females. This bird is common in thornveld and broadleaved woodlands. A ground feeder, it walks with short steps in search of insects and seeds. These birds sing a whistled 'weechee, weechee, weechee' from a perch in a tree.

ROOIRUGSTREEPKOPPIE (884)

Die Rooirugstreepkoppie kan uitgeken word aan sy kastaiingbruin mantel, swart-en-wit gestreepte kop en goudgeel bors, wat helderder is by mannetjies as by wyfies. Hulle vreet op die grond en loop met klein treetjies op soek na insekte en sade. Hierdie voël sing 'weetjee-weetjee-weetjee' van 'n sitplek in 'n boom. Hulle kom algemeen voor in doringveld en breëblaarboswêreld.

LE BRUANT A POITRINE DOREE (884)

On identifie le bruant à poitrine dorée par le manteau châtain, la tête striée noire et blanche, et pat la poitrine jaune dorée, plus vive aux mâles. Fréquent et répandu, cet oiseau trouve à l'épine, aux plantations exotiques et au pays boisé à larges feuilles. Mangeur par terre, il marche à petits pas pour trouver des insectes et des graines. Il chante 'weechee, weechee, weechee', sifflant d'un perchoir dans un arbre.

GELBBAUCHAMMER (884)

Die Gelbbauchammer erkennt man an ihrem kastanienbraunen Rückengefieder, dem schwarzweißgestreiften Kopf und der goldgelben Brust, die beim Männchen leuchtender ist als beim Weibchen. Diese Vögel kommen häufig in der Dornsavanne und im breitblättrigen Waldland vor. Bei der Nahrungsaufnahme, das heißt auf der Suche nach Insekten und Samen, trippeln sie auf dem Boden herum. Sie trillern ihr 'Wietschi-Wietschi-Wietschi' aus dem Baumgipfel.

Emberiza flaviventris

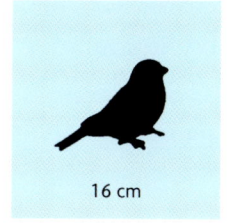

16 cm

ADDO ELEPHANT,
KRUGER,
MARAKELE

INDEX